100 Days
of
Prayer
Daily Devotional

STEPHEN ARTERBURN

100 DAYS OF PRAYER

Book cover and layout design by Sergio Urquiza & Cristalle Kishi

ISBN: 9781628624281

Printed through Asia Pacific Offset Ltd
Printed in China
February 2018, 1st Printing

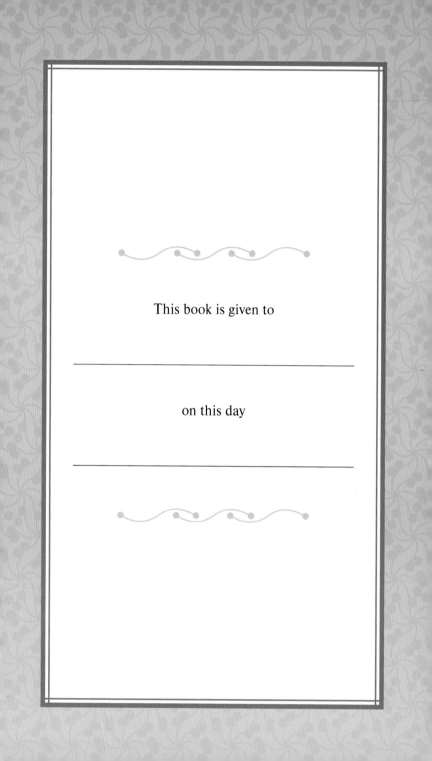

This book is given to

on this day

Contents

Introduction 7
DAY 1: Prayer Changes Things and You 8
DAY 2: Asking for Directions 10
DAY 3: This Is His Day 12
DAY 4: An Attitude of Gratitude 14
DAY 5: Discovering God's Plans 16
DAY 6: Christ's Love Changes Everything 18
DAY 7: The Power of Prayer 20
DAY 8: Not Enough Hours? 22
DAY 9: Taking Up the Cross 24
DAY 10: A Fresh Opportunity 26
DAY 11: Courage for the Journey 28
DAY 12: Faith for Life 30
DAY 13: Measuring Your Words 32
DAY 14: The Greatest of These 34
DAY 15: God's Guidance 36
DAY 16: His Promises 38
DAY 17: Let the Celebration Begin 40
DAY 18: Ultimate Accountability 42
DAY 19: The Self-Fulfilling Prophecy 44
DAY 20: Infinite Possibilities 46
DAY 21: Contagious Faith 48
DAY 22: An Intensely Bright Future: Yours 50
DAY 23: The Fullness of Christ 52
DAY 24: In Times of Adversity 54
DAY 25: Seeking God and Finding Happiness 56
DAY 26: God's Guidebook 58
DAY 27: Too Busy? 60
DAY 28: Always with Us 62
DAY 29: Relying upon Him 64
DAY 30: Growing in Christ 66
DAY 31: Honoring God 68

DAY 32: Beyond Guilt 70

DAY 33: We Belong to Him 72

DAY 34: He Is Here 74

DAY 35: The Lessons of Tough Times 76

DAY 36: Give Me Patience, Lord, Right Now!............78

DAY 37: The World's Best Friend...............................80

DAY 38: A Godly Leader 82

DAY 39: The Wisdom of Moderation 84

DAY 40: Look Up and Move On 86

DAY 41: The Voice Inside Your Head 88

DAY 42: Encouraging Words for Family and Friends...........90

DAY 43: Your Traveling Companion...........................92

DAY 44: Life Eternal..94

DAY 45: Forgive: It's God's Way.................................96

DAY 46: Neighbors in Need.......................................98

DAY 47: Your Real Riches...100

DAY 48: Real Repentance 102

DAY 49: Conquering Everyday Frustrations 104

DAY 50: God's Timetable 106

DAY 51: Roadmap for Life 108

DAY 52: Actions That Reflect Our Beliefs 110

DAY 53: The Right Kind of Behavior........................112

DAY 54: His Rule, Your Rule.....................................114

DAY 55: Enthusiasm for Christ.................................116

DAY 56: Outgrowing Bad Habits..............................118

DAY 57: He Overcomes 120

DAY 58: The Temptation to Judge 122

DAY 59: The World . . . and You 124

DAY 60: Using God's Gifts.......................................126

DAY 61: You Are Blessed..128

DAY 62: Cheerfulness 101..130

DAY 63: Let God Decide 132

DAY 64: The Remedy for Uncertainty......................134

DAY 65: Thanksgiving Yes . . . Envy No! 136

DAY 66: Walking in His Footsteps 138

DAY 67: In His Hands 140

DAY 68: Obey and Be Blessed 142

DAY 69: The Love of Money.........................144

DAY 70: He Offers Peace 146

DAY 71: Constant Praise 148

DAY 72: The Shepherd's Gift 150

DAY 73: He Renews Our Strength 152

DAY 74: Sharing the Good News 154

DAY 75: Temporary Setbacks......................156

DAY 76: The Morning Watch.......................158

DAY 77: Wisdom in a Donut Shop 160

DAY 78: Pleasing God................................162

DAY 79: A God-Made Man...........................164

DAY 80: When People Behave Badly 166

DAY 81: Acceptance Today 168

DAY 82: Choosing Wisely..........................170

DAY 83: Confident Christianity 172

DAY 84: Genuine Contentment...................174

DAY 85: A Book Unlike Any Other...............176

DAY 86: Shouting the Good News................178

DAY 87: A Life of Fulfillment......................180

DAY 88: God Is Love 182

DAY 89: We Are All Role Models 184

DAY 90: Heeding God's Call 186

DAY 91: Becoming Wise.............................188

DAY 92: Beyond Worry..............................190

DAY 93: Making Peace with Your Past..........192

DAY 94: His Perspective . . . and Yours.........194

DAY 95: Solving Problems..........................196

DAY 96: Beyond Bitterness 198

DAY 97: Unbending Truth 200

DAY 98: A Series of Choices 202

DAY 99: Focusing on God 204

DAY 100: Commissioned to Witness 206

Introduction

Each day provides opportunities to put God where he belongs—at the center of our lives. When we do so, we worship him, not only with our words and deeds, but also with our prayers.

This text contains 100 devotional readings that are intended to remind you of the need for prayer and the power of prayer. And the ideas in this book are also intended to remind you of the eternal promises that are found in God's Holy Word.

For the next 100 days, try this experiment: Read a chapter a day and internalize the ideas that you find here. If you're already committed to a daily worship time, this book will enrich that experience. If you are not, the simple act of giving God a few minutes each morning will change the direction and the quality of your life.

If you're facing a powerful temptation or a seemingly insoluble problem, don't give up and don't stop praying. Instead, keep searching for direction—God's direction. And while you're at it, keep searching for perspective and wisdom—starting with God's wisdom. When you do, you'll discover the comfort, the power, and the peace that only he can give.

Prayer Changes Things and You

If you believe, you will receive whatever you ask for in prayer.

MATTHEW 21:22

I s prayer an integral part of your daily life, or is it a hit-or-miss habit? Do you "pray without ceasing," or is your prayer life an afterthought? Do you regularly pray in the solitude of the early morning darkness, or do you lower your head only when others are watching? The answer to these questions will determine the direction of your day—and your life.

So here's your challenge: During the next 100 days, make yourself a prayer warrior. Begin your prayers early in the morning and continue them throughout the day. And remember: God does answer your prayers, but he's not likely to answer those prayers until you've prayed them.

You don't need fancy words or religious phrases. Just tell God the way it really is.

JIM CYMBALA

We must pray literally without ceasing, in every occurrence and employment of our lives. You know I mean that prayer of the heart which is independent of place or situation, or which is, rather, a habit of lifting up the heart to God, as in a constant communication with Him.

ELIZABETH ANN SETON

I need the spiritual revival that comes from spending quiet time alone with Jesus in prayer and in thoughtful meditation on His Word.

ANNE GRAHAM LOTZ

TODAY'S PRAYER

I pray to you, my heavenly Father,
because you desire it and because I need it.
Prayer not only changes things; it changes me.
Help me, Lord, never to face the demands of the
day without first spending time with you.

Amen.

ASKING FOR DIRECTIONS

If any of you lacks wisdom, you should ask God,
who gives generously to all without finding fault,
and it will be given to you.

JAMES 1:5

Genuine, heartfelt prayer produces powerful changes in us and in our world. When we lift our hearts to God, we open ourselves to a never-ending source of divine wisdom and infinite love. Jesus made it clear to his disciples that they should petition God to meet their needs. So should we.

- Do you have questions about your future that you simply can't answer?

- Do you have needs that you simply can't meet by yourself?

- Do you sincerely seek to know God's unfolding plans for your life?

If so, ask him for direction, for protection, and for strength—and then keep asking him every day that you live. Whatever your need, no matter how great or small, pray about it and have faith. God is not just near; he is here, and he's perfectly capable of answering your prayers. Now, it's up to you to ask.

God makes prayer as easy as possible for us. He's completely approachable and available, and He'll never mock or upbraid us for bringing our needs before Him.

SHIRLEY DOBSON

Prayer moves the arm that moves the world.

ANNIE ARMSTRONG

Rest assured: Do what God tells you to do now, and, depend upon it, you will be shown what to do next.

ELISABETH ELLIOT

TODAY'S PRAYER

Lord, when I have questions about my purpose in life, I will turn to you. When I am weak, I will seek your strength. When I am discouraged, Father, I will be mindful of your love and your grace. I will ask you for the things I need, Father, and I will trust your answers, today and forever.

Amen.

THIS IS HIS DAY

The LORD has done it this very day;
let us rejoice today and be glad.

PSALM 118:24

God gives us this day; he fills it to the brim with possibilities, and he challenges us to use it for his purposes. The 118th Psalm reminds us that today, like every other day, is a cause for celebration. The day is presented to us fresh and clean at midnight, free of charge, but we must beware: Today is a non-renewable resource—once it's gone, it's gone forever. Our responsibility, of course, is to use this day in the service of God's will and according to his commandments.

Today, treasure the time that God has given you. Give him the glory and the praise and the thanksgiving that he deserves. And search for the hidden possibilities that God has placed along your path. This day is a priceless gift from God, so use it joyfully and encourage others to do likewise. Rejoice and be glad!

All our life is a celebration for us; we are convinced, in fact, that God is always everywhere. We sing while we work . . . we pray while we carry out all life's other occupations.

ST. CLEMENT OF ALEXANDRIA

Some of us seem so anxious about avoiding hell that we forget to celebrate our journey toward heaven.

PHILIP YANCEY

If you can forgive the person you were, accept the person you are, and believe in the person you will become, you are headed for joy. So celebrate your life.

BARBARA JOHNSON

TODAY'S PRAYER

Dear Lord, you have given me so many blessings, and as a way of saying "Thank you," I will celebrate. I will be a joyful Christian, Lord, quick to smile and slow to frown. And, I will share my joy with my family, with my friends, and with my neighbors, this day and every day.

Amen.

An Attitude
of Gratitude

Finally, brothers and sisters, whatever is true,
whatever is noble, whatever is right, whatever is pure,
whatever is lovely, whatever is admirable—if anything
is excellent or praiseworthy—think about such things.

PHILIPPIANS 4:8

How will you direct your thoughts today?

- Will you obey the words of Philippians 4:8 by dwelling upon those things that are true, noble, right, pure, lovely, and admirable?

- Or will you allow your thoughts to be hijacked by the negativity that seems to dominate our troubled world?

- Are you fearful, angry, bored, or worried?

- Are you so preoccupied with the concerns of this day that you fail to thank God for the promise of eternity?

- Are you confused, bitter, or pessimistic?

If so, God wants to have a little talk with you.

God intends that you experience joy and abundance. So, today and every day hereafter, celebrate the life that God has given you by focusing your thoughts upon those things that are worthy of praise. Today, count your blessings instead of your hardships. And thank God, the giver of all things good, for gifts that are simply too numerous to count.

"If the Lord will" is not just a statement on a believer's lips; it is the constant attitude of his heart.

WARREN WIERSBE

When we were children we were grateful to those who filled our stockings at Christmas time. Why are we not grateful to God for filling our stockings with legs?

G.K. CHESTERTON

God doesn't bless us just to make us happy; He blesses us to make us a blessing.

WARREN WIERSBE

TODAY'S PRAYER

Dear Lord, help me have an attitude
that is pleasing to you as I count my blessings
today, tomorrow, and every day.

Amen.

DISCOVERING GOD'S PLANS

*For it is God who works in you to will and to act
in order to fulfill his good purpose.*

PHILIPPIANS 2:13

I f you seek to live in accordance with God's will for your life—and you should—then you will live in accordance with his commandments. You will study God's Word, and you will be watchful for his signs. You will associate with fellow Christians who will encourage your spiritual growth, and you will listen to that inner voice that speaks to you in the quiet moments of your daily devotionals.

God intends to use you in wonderful, unexpected ways if you let him. The decision to seek God's plan and to follow it is yours and yours alone. The consequences of that decision have implications that are both profound and eternal, so choose carefully.

God has a plan for the life of every Christian. Every circumstance, every turn of destiny, all things work together for your good and for His glory.

—Billy Graham

If not a sparrow falls upon the ground without your Father, you have reason to see that the smallest events of your career and your life are arranged by him.

C. H. Spurgeon

God is preparing you as his chosen arrow. As yet your shaft is hidden in his quiver, in the shadows, but, at the precise moment, he will reach for you and launch you to that place of his appointment.

Charles Swindoll

Today's Prayer

Dear Lord, you created me for a reason. Give me the wisdom to follow your direction for my life's journey. Let me do your work here on earth by seeking your will and living it, knowing that when I trust in you, Father, I am eternally blessed.

Amen.

CHRIST'S LOVE CHANGES EVERYTHING

For you died, and your life is now hidden with Christ in God.

COLOSSIANS 3:3

Christ's love is perfect and steadfast. Even though we are fallible and wayward, the Good Shepherd cares for us still.

What does the love of Christ mean to his believers? It changes everything. Even though we have fallen far short of the Father's commandments, Christ loves us with a power and depth that is beyond our understanding.

And, as we accept Christ's love and walk in Christ's footsteps, our lives bear testimony to his power and to his grace. Yes, Christ's love changes everything; may we invite him into our hearts so it can then change everything in us.

Jesus is all compassion. He never betrays us.

CATHERINE MARSHALL

Live your lives in love, the same sort of love which Christ gives us, and which He perfectly expressed when He gave Himself as a sacrifice to God.

CORRIE TEN BOOM

So Jesus came, stripping himself of everything as he came—omnipotence, omniscience, omnipresence—everything except love. . . . Love—his only protection, his only weapon, his only method.

E. STANLEY JONES

He loved us not because we're lovable, but because He is love.

C. S. LEWIS

TODAY'S PRAYER

Dear Jesus, my life has been changed forever by your love and sacrifice. Today I will praise you, I will honor you, and I will walk with you.

Amen.

THE POWER OF PRAYER

*Therefore confess your sins to each other and pray for
each other so that you may be healed. The prayer of a
righteous person is powerful and effective.*

JAMES 5:16

Prayer is a powerful tool for communicating with our Creator; it is an opportunity to commune with the giver of all things good. *The power of prayer—* these words are so familiar, yet sometimes we forget what they mean. Prayer helps us find strength for today and hope for the future. Prayer is not a thing to be taken lightly or to be used infrequently.

The quality of your spiritual life will be in direct proportion to the quality of your prayer life. Prayer changes things, and it changes you. Today, instead of turning things over in your mind, turn them over to God in prayer. Instead of worrying about your next decision, ask God to lead the way. Pray constantly about things great and small. God is listening, and he wants to hear from you now.

Is prayer your steering wheel or your spare tire?

CORRIE TEN BOOM

Prayer may not change things for you, but it for sure changes you for things.

SAMUEL M. SHOEMAKER

Prayer is the most important tool for your mission to the world. People may refuse our love or reject our message, but they are defenseless against our prayers.

RICK WARREN

TODAY'S PRAYER

Dear Lord, let me raise my hopes and my dreams, my worries and my fears to you. Let me be a worthy example to family and friends, showing them the importance and the power of prayer. Let me take everything to you in prayer, Lord, and when I do, let me trust in your answers.

Amen.

Not Enough Hours?

It is good to praise the LORD and make music to your name, O Most High, proclaiming your love in the morning and your faithfulness at night.

PSALM 92:1–2

If you ever find that you're simply "too busy" for a daily chat with your Father in heaven, it's time to take a long, hard look at your priorities and your values. Each day has 1,440 minutes—do you value your relationship with God enough to spend a few of those minutes with him? He deserves that much of your time and more—is he receiving it from you? Hopefully so.

As you consider your plans for the day ahead, here's a tip: Organize your life around the simple principle of putting God first. When you place your Creator where he belongs—at the very center of your day and your life—the rest of your priorities will fall into place.

A person with no devotional life generally struggles with faith and obedience.

CHARLES STANLEY

This day's bustle and hurly-burly would too often and too soon call us away from Jesus' feet. These distractions must be immediately dismissed, or we shall know only the "barrenness of busyness."

A. W. TOZER

The busier we are, the easier it is to worry, the greater the temptation to worry, the greater the need to be alone with God.

CHARLES STANLEY

There is an enormous power in little things to distract our attention from God.

OSWALD CHAMBERS

TODAY'S PRAYER

Dear Lord, every day of my life is a journey with you. I will take time today to think, to pray, and to study your Word. Guide my steps, Father, and keep me mindful that today offers yet another opportunity to celebrate your blessings, your love, and your Son.

Amen.

TAKING UP THE CROSS

*Then he said to them all: "Whoever wants to be my
disciple must deny themselves and take up their
cross daily and follow me.*

LUKE 9:23

When Jesus addressed his disciples, he warned
them that each one must, "take up his cross
daily, and follow me." Christ's message was
clear: In order to follow him, Christ's disciples must deny
themselves and, instead, trust him completely. Nothing
has changed since then.

When we have been saved by Christ, we can, if we choose,
become passive Christians. We can sit back, secure in our
own salvation, and let other believers spread the healing
message of Jesus. But instead, we are commanded to
become disciples of the One who has saved us.

Do you seek to fulfill God's purpose for your life? Then
follow Christ. Follow him by picking up his cross today
and every day that you live. Then, you will quickly
discover that Christ's love has the power to change
everything, including you.

Discipleship means personal, passionate devotion to a person, our Lord Jesus Christ.

OSWALD CHAMBERS

There is not Christianity without a cross, for you cannot be a disciple of Jesus without taking up your cross.

HENRY BLACKABY

If we would be followers of Christ, indeed we must become personally and vitally involved in His death and resurrection. And this requires repentance, prayer, watchfulness, self-denial, detachment from the world, humility, obedience, and cross carrying.

A. W. TOZER

TODAY'S PRAYER

Help me, Lord, to understand what cross I am to bear this day. Give me the strength and the courage to carry that cross along the path of your choosing so that I may be a worthy disciple of your Son.

Amen.

A Fresh Opportunity

We were therefore buried with him through baptism
into death in order that, just as Christ was raised from
the dead through the glory of the Father,
we too may live a new life.

ROMANS 6:4

Each morning offers a fresh opportunity to invite Christ, yet once again, to rule over our hearts and our days. Each morning presents yet another opportunity to take up his cross and follow in his footsteps.

God's Word is clear. When we genuinely invite him to reign over our hearts, and when we accept his transforming love, we are forever changed. When we welcome Christ into our hearts, an old life ends and a new way of living—along with a completely new way of viewing the world—begins.

Today, let us rejoice in the new life that is ours through Christ, and let us follow him, step by step, on the path that he first walked.

No man is ever the same after God has laid His hand upon him.

A. W. Tozer

The transforming love of God has repositioned me for eternity. I am now a new man, forgiven, basking in the warm love of our living God, trusting His promises and provision, and enjoying life to the fullest.

Bill Bright

Turn your life over to Christ today, and your life will never be the same.

Billy Graham

Today's Prayer

Heavenly Father, renew in me the passion to share the good news of Jesus Christ. Make the experience of my conversion real and fresh so that I might be an effective witness for you.

Amen.

COURAGE FOR THE JOURNEY

*Jesus immediately said to them:
"Take courage! It is I. Don't be afraid."*

MATTHEW 14:27

A storm rose quickly on the Sea of Galilee, and the disciples were afraid. Although they had seen Jesus perform many miracles, the disciples feared for their lives, so they turned to their Savior, and he calmed the waters and the wind.

Sometimes, we, like the disciples, feel threatened by the inevitable storms of life. And when we are fearful, we, too, can turn to Christ for courage and for comfort.

The next time you're afraid, remember that the One who calmed the wind and the waves is also your personal Savior. And remember that the ultimate battle has already been won at Calvary. We, as believers, can live courageously in the promises of our Lord . . . and we should.

The fear of God is the death of every other fear.

C. H. SPURGEON

Down through the centuries, in times of trouble and trial, God has brought courage to the hearts of those who love Him. The Bible is filled with assurances of God's help and comfort in every kind of trouble.

BILLY GRAHAM

To fear and not be afraid, that is the paradox of faith.

A. W. TOZER

What is courage? It is the ability to be strong in trust, in conviction, in obedience. To be courageous is to step out in faith—to trust and obey, no matter what.

KAY ARTHUR

TODAY'S PRAYER

Dear Lord, sometimes I face disappointments
and challenges that leave me worried and afraid.
When I am fearful, let me seek your strength.
Keep me mindful, Lord, that you are my God.
With you by my side, Lord, I have nothing to fear.
Help me to be your grateful and courageous
servant this day and every day.

Amen.

FAITH FOR LIFE

For everyone born of God overcomes the world.
This is the victory that has overcome
the world, even our faith.

1 JOHN 5:4

Take a moment and carefully consider the following question: Do you desire the abundance and success that God has promised?

The first element of a successful life is faith—faith in God, faith in his Son, and faith in his promises. If we place our lives in God's hands, our faith is rewarded in ways that we—as human beings with clouded vision and limited understanding—can scarcely comprehend. But, if we seek to rely solely upon our own resources, or if we seek earthly success outside the boundaries of God's commandments, we reap a bitter harvest for ourselves and for our loved ones.

Trust God today and every day that you live. Then, when you have entrusted your future to the giver of all things good, rest assured that your future is secure, not only for today, but also for all eternity.

Faith is seeing light with the eyes of your heart, when the eyes of your body see only darkness.

BARBARA JOHNSON

Faith, as Paul saw it, was a living, flaming thing leading to surrender and obedience to the commandments of Christ.

A. W. TOZER

We have ample evidence that the Lord is able to guide. The promises cover every imaginable situation. All we need to do is to take the hand he stretches out.

ELISABETH ELLIOT

TODAY'S PRAYER

Father, in the dark moments of my life, help me to remember that you are always near and that you can overcome any challenge. Keep me mindful of your love and your power, so that I may live courageously and faithfully today and every day.

Amen.

Measuring Your Words

The hearts of the wise make their mouths prudent,
and their lips promote instruction.

Proverbs 16:23

I f you seek to be a source of encouragement to friends, to family members, and to coworkers, then you must measure your words carefully. And that's exactly what God wants you to do. God's Word reminds us that "The words of the reckless pierce like swords, but the tongue of the wise brings healing" (Proverbs 12:18).

Today, make this promise to yourself: vow to be an honest, effective, encouraging communicator at work, at home, and everyplace in between. Speak wisely, not impulsively. Use words of kindness and praise, not words of anger or derision. Learn how to be truthful without being cruel. Remember that you have the power to heal others or to injure them, to lift others up or to hold them back. And when you learn how to lift them up, you'll soon discover that you've lifted yourself up, too.

Part of good communication is listening with the eyes as well as with the ears.

JOSH MCDOWELL

We should ask ourselves three things before we speak: Is it true? Is it kind? Does it glorify God?

BILLY GRAHAM

Attitude and the spirit in which we communicate are as important as the words we say.

CHARLES STANLEY

TODAY'S PRAYER

Lord, you have warned me that I will be judged by
the words I speak. Keep me mindful,
Lord, that I have influence on many people;
make me an influence for good.
And, may the words that I speak today be worthy
of the One who has saved me forever.

Amen.

THE GREATEST OF THESE

These three remain: faith, hope and love.
But the greatest of these is love.

1 CORINTHIANS 13:13

We are commanded (not advised, not encouraged . . . commanded!) to love one another just as Christ loved us (see John 13:34). The beautiful words of First Corinthians 13 remind us that love is God's commandment. Faith is important, of course. So, too, is hope. But, love is more important still. That's a tall order, but as Christians, we are obligated to follow it.

Christ showed his love for us on the cross, and we are called upon to return Christ's love by sharing it. Today, let us spread Christ's love to families, friends, and even strangers, so that through us, others might come to know him.

Christian love, either towards God or towards man, is an affair of the will.

C. S. LEWIS

The cross symbolizes a cosmic as well as a historic truth. Love conquers the world, but its victory is not an easy one.

REINHOLD NEIBUHR

You can be sure you are abiding in Christ if you are able to have a Christlike love toward the people that irritate you the most.

VONETTE BRIGHT

Suppose that I understand the Bible. And, suppose that I am the greatest preacher who ever lived! The Apostle Paul wrote that unless I have love, "I am nothing."

BILLY GRAHAM

TODAY'S PRAYER

Lord, love is your commandment.
Help me always to remember that the gift of love is a precious gift indeed. Let me nurture love and treasure it, today and forever.

Amen.

GOD'S GUIDANCE

*The LORD makes firm the steps of the one
who delights in him.*

PSALM 37:23

ant to know a great truth about God? God is intensely interested in each of us, and he will guide our steps if we serve him obediently.

When we sincerely offer heartfelt prayers to our heavenly Father, he will give direction and meaning to our lives—but he won't force us to follow him. To the contrary, God has given us the free will to follow his commandments . . . or not.

When we stray from God's commandments, we invite bitter consequences. But, when we follow his commandments, and when we genuinely and humbly seek his will, he touches our hearts and leads us on the path of his choosing.

Will you trust God to guide your steps? You should. When you entrust your life to him completely and without reservation, God will give you the strength to meet any challenge, the courage to face any trial, and the wisdom to live in his righteousness and in his peace. So trust him today and seek his guidance. When you do, your next step will be the right one.

A spiritual discipline is necessary in order to move slowly from an absurd to an obedient life, from a life filled with noisy worries to a life in which there is some free inner space where we can listen to our God and follow his guidance.

HENRI NOUWEN

Only He can guide you to invest your life in worthwhile ways. This guidance will come as you "walk" with Him and listen to Him.

HENRY BLACKABY AND CLAUDE KING

I don't doubt that the Holy Spirit guides your decisions from within when you make them with the intention of pleasing God. The error would be to think that He speaks only within, whereas in reality He speaks also through Scripture, the Church, Christian friends, and books.

C. S. LEWIS

TODAY'S PRAYER

Dear Lord, you always stand ready to guide me.
Let me accept your guidance, today and every day
of my life. Lead me, Father, so that my life
can be a tribute to your grace, to your mercy,
to your love, and to your Son.

Amen.

His Promises

Let us hold unswervingly to the hope we profess,
for he who promised is faithful.

Hebrews 10:23

The Christian faith is founded upon promises that are contained in a unique book. That book is the Holy Bible. The Bible is a roadmap for life here on earth and for life eternal. As Christians, we are called upon to study its meaning, to trust its promises, to follow its commandments, and to share its good news. God's Holy Word is, indeed, a transforming, life-changing, one-of-a-kind treasure. And, a passing acquaintance with the Good Book is insufficient for Christians who seek to obey God's Word and understand his will.

God has made promises to you, and he intends to keep them. So take God at his word: trust his promises and share them with your family, with your friends, and with the world.

We can have full confidence in God's promises because we can have full faith in His character.

FRANKLIN GRAHAM

There are four words I wish we would never forget, and they are, "God keeps his word."

CHARLES SWINDOLL

The stars may fall, but God's promises will stand and be fulfilled.

J. I. PACKER

TODAY'S PRAYER

Lord, your Holy Word contains promises, and I will trust them. I will use the Bible as my guide, and I will trust you, Lord, to speak to me through your Holy Spirit and through your Holy Word, this day and forever.

Amen.

LET THE CELEBRATION BEGIN

*I have told you this so that my joy may be in you
and that your joy may be complete.*

JOHN 15:11

Oswald Chambers correctly observed, "Joy is the great note all throughout the Bible." C. S. Lewis echoed that thought when he wrote, "Joy is the serious business of heaven." But, even the most dedicated Christians can, on occasion, forget to celebrate each day for what it is: a priceless gift from God.

Today, let us be joyful Christians with smiles on our faces and kind words on our lips. After all, this is God's day, and he has given us clear instructions for its use. We are commanded to rejoice and be glad. So, with no further ado, let the celebration begin!

When Jesus Christ is the source of our joy, no words can describe it.

BILLY GRAHAM

Joy is the direct result of having God's perspective on our daily lives and the effect of loving our Lord enough to obey His commands and trust His promises.

BILL BRIGHT

You have to look for the joy. Look for the light of God that is hitting your life, and you will find sparkles you didn't know were there.

BARBARA JOHNSON

TODAY'S PRAYER

Dear Lord, you have given me so many blessings; let me celebrate your gifts. Make me thankful, loving, responsible, and wise. Make me be a joyful Christian, a worthy example to others, and a dutiful servant to you this day and forever.

Amen.

ULTIMATE ACCOUNTABILITY

*Encouraging, comforting and urging you
to live lives worthy of God, who calls you
into his kingdom and glory.*

1 THESSALONIANS 2:12

For most of us, it is a daunting thought: One day, perhaps soon, we'll come face-to-face with our heavenly Father, and we'll be called to account for our actions here on earth. Our personal histories will certainly not be surprising to God; he already knows everything about us. But the full scope of our activities may be surprising to us. Some of us will be pleasantly surprised; others will not be.

Today, do whatever you can to ensure that your thoughts and your deeds are pleasing to your Creator. Because you will, at some point in the future, be called to account for your actions. And the future may be sooner than you think.

The temptation of the age is to look good without being good.

BRENNAN MANNING

The Bible teaches that we are accountable to one another for our conduct and character.

CHARLES STANLEY

We can always gauge where we are by the teachings of Jesus Christ.

OSWALD CHAMBERS

The best evidence of our having the truth is our walking in the truth.

MATTHEW HENRY

TODAY'S PRAYER

Dear Lord, let my words and actions show the world the changes that you have made in my life. You sent your Son so that I might have abundant life and eternal life. Thank you, Father, for my Savior, Christ Jesus. I will follow him, honor him, and share his good news, this day and every day.

Amen.

THE SELF-FULFILLING PROPHECY

*May he give you the desire of your heart
and make all your plans succeed.*

PSALM 20:4

T he self-fulfilling prophecy is alive, well, and living at your house. If you trust God and have faith for the future, your optimistic beliefs will give you direction and motivation. That's one reason that you should never lose hope, but certainly not the only reason. The primary reason that you, as a believer, should never lose hope, is because of God's unfailing promises.

Make no mistake about it: Thoughts are powerful things. Your thoughts have the power to lift you up or to hold you down. When you acquire the habit of hopeful thinking, you will have acquired a powerful tool for improving your life. So if you fall into the habit of negative thinking, think again. After all, God's Word teaches us that Christ can overcome every difficulty (John 16:33). And when God makes a promise, he keeps it.

Our hope in Christ for the future is the mainstream of our joy.

C. H. SPURGEON

What oxygen is to the lungs, such is hope to the meaning of life.

EMIL BRUNNER

Oh, remember this: There is never a time when we may not hope in God. Whatever our necessities, however great our difficulties, and though to all appearance help is impossible, yet our business is to hope in God, and it will be found that it is not in vain.

GEORGE MÜLLER

I wish I could make it all new again; I can't. But God can. "He restores my soul," wrote the shepherd. God doesn't reform; he restores. He doesn't camouflage the old; he restores the new. The Master Builder will pull out the original plan and restore it. He will restore the vigor, he will restore the energy. He will restore the hope. He will restore the soul.

MAX LUCADO

TODAY'S PRAYER

Dear Lord, make me a hope-filled Christian. If I become discouraged, let me turn to you. If I grow weary, let me seek strength in you. In every aspect of my life, I will trust you, Father, today and forever.

Amen.

Infinite Possibilities

Is anything too hard for the Lord?

Genesis 18:14

A re you afraid to ask God to do big things in your life? Is your faith threadbare and worn? If so, it's time to abandon your doubts and reclaim your faith in God's promises.

Ours is a God of infinite possibilities. But sometimes, because of limited faith and limited understanding, we wrongly assume that God cannot or will not intervene in the affairs of humankind. Such assumptions are simply wrong.

God's Holy Word makes it clear that absolutely nothing is impossible for the Lord. And since the Bible means what it says, you can be comforted in the knowledge that the Creator of the universe can do miraculous things in your own life and in the lives of your loved ones. Your challenge, as a believer, is to take God at his word, and to expect the miraculous.

You can believe in the Holy Spirit not because you see Him, but because you see what He does in people's lives when they are surrendered to Christ and possess His power.

BILLY GRAHAM

The most profane word we use is "hopeless." When you say a situation or person is hopeless, you are slamming the door in the face of God.

KATHY TROCCOLI

There is Someone who makes possible what seems completely impossible.

CATHERINE MARSHALL

TODAY'S PRAYER

Dear God, nothing is impossible for you. Keep me always mindful of your strength. When I lose hope, give me faith; when others lose hope, let me tell them of your glory and your works. Today, Lord, let me expect the miraculous, and let me trust in you.

Amen.

CONTAGIOUS FAITH

Whatever you do, work at it with all your heart,
as working for the LORD, not for human masters.

COLOSSIANS 3:23

Are you genuinely excited about your faith? And do you make your enthusiasm known to those around you? Or are you a "silent ambassador" for Christ? God's preference is clear: He intends that you stand before others and proclaim your faith.

Genuine, heartfelt Christianity is contagious. If you enjoy a life-altering relationship with God, that relationship will have an impact on others—perhaps a profound impact.

Does Christ reign over your life? Then share your testimony and your excitement. The world needs both.

Prayer must be aflame. Prayer without fervor is as a sun without light or heat, or as a flower without beauty or fragrance. A soul devoted to God is a fervent soul, and prayer is the creature of that flame. He only can truly pray who is all aglow for holiness, for God, and for heaven.

E. M. Bounds

Catch on fire with enthusiasm and people will come for miles to watch you burn.

John Wesley

Don't take hold of a thing unless you want that thing to take hold of you.

E. Stanley Jones

Today's Prayer

Dear Lord, I know that others are watching the way that I live my life. Help me to be an enthusiastic Christian with a faith that is contagious.

Amen.

An Intensely Bright Future: Yours

Now to him who is able to do immeasurably more than all we ask or imagine, according to his power that is at work within us.

EPHESIANS 3:20

I t takes courage to dream big dreams. You will discover that courage when you do three things: accept the past, trust God to handle the future, and make the most of the time he has given you today.

- Are you excited about the opportunities of today and thrilled by the possibilities of tomorrow?

- Do you confidently expect God to lead you to a place of abundance, peace, and joy?

- When your days on earth are over, do you expect to receive the priceless gift of eternal life?

If you trust God's promises, and if you have welcomed God's Son into your heart, then you should believe that your future is intensely and eternally bright.

No dreams are too big for God—not even yours. So start living—and dreaming—accordingly.

The biggest human temptation is to settle for too little.

THOMAS MERTON

The future lies all before us. Shall it only be a slight advance upon what we usually do? Ought it not to be a bound, a leap forward to altitudes of endeavor and success undreamed of before?

ANNIE ARMSTRONG

There is no magic in small plans. When I consider my ministry, I think of the world. Anything less than that would not be worthy of Christ nor of His will for my life.

HENRIETTA C. MEARS

TODAY'S PRAYER

Dear Lord, my hope is in you.
Give me the courage to face the future with certainty, and give me the wisdom to follow in the footsteps of your Son, today and forever.

Amen.

The Fullness of Christ

*I have come that they may have life,
and have it to the full.*

John 10:10

The tenth chapter of John tells us that Christ came to earth so that our lives might be lived "to the full." But what, exactly, did Jesus mean? Was he talking about a life filled with material possessions or financial wealth?

Hardly. Jesus offers a different kind of fullness of life: a spiritual richness that extends beyond the temporal boundaries of this world. This everlasting fullness is available to all who seek it and claim it.

May we, as believers, claim the riches of Christ Jesus every day that we live, and may we share his blessings with all who cross our path.

The only way you can experience abundant life is to surrender your plans to Him.

CHARLES STANLEY

The man who lives without Jesus is the poorest of the poor, whereas no one is so rich as the man who lives in His grace.

THOMAS À KEMPIS

If you want purpose and meaning and satisfaction and fulfillment and peace and hope and joy and abundant life that lasts forever, look to Jesus.

ANNE GRAHAM LOTZ

TODAY'S PRAYER

Dear Lord, you have offered me the gift of a full life through your Son. Thank you, Father, for the life that is mine through Christ Jesus. Let me accept his gifts and use them always to glorify you.

Amen.

In Times of Adversity

For everyone born of God overcomes the world.
This is the victory that has overcome the world,
even our faith.

1 John 5:4

When we face the inevitable difficulties of life here on earth, God stands ready to protect us. All of us face times of adversity. On occasion, we all must endure the disappointments and tragedies that befall believers and nonbelievers alike. The reassuring words of 1 John 5:4 remind us that when we accept God's grace, we overcome the passing hardships of this world by relying upon his strength, his love, and his promise of eternal life.

When we call upon God in heartfelt prayer, he will answer—in his own time and according to his own plan—and he will heal us. And while we are waiting for God's plans to unfold and for his healing touch to restore us, we can be comforted in the knowledge that our Creator can overcome any obstacle, even if we cannot. Let us take God at his word, and let us trust him today . . . and every day.

God will make obstacles serve His purpose.

MRS. CHARLES E. COWMAN

Adversity is always unexpected and unwelcomed.
It is an intruder and a thief, and yet in the hands of
God, adversity becomes the means through which His
supernatural power is demonstrated.

CHARLES STANLEY

God will not permit any troubles to come upon us unless
He has a specific plan by which great blessing can come
out of the difficulty.

PETER MARSHALL

TODAY'S PRAYER

Dear heavenly Father, when I am troubled, you heal
me. When I am afraid, you protect me. When I am
discouraged, you lift me up. In times of adversity,
let me trust your plan and your will for my life.
And whatever my circumstances, Lord, let me
always give the thanks and the glory to you.

Amen.

SEEKING GOD AND FINDING HAPPINESS

Blessed are those whose . . .
hope is in the LORD their God.

PSALM 146:5

D o you sincerely want to be a happy Christian? Then set your mind and your heart upon God's love and his grace.

Happiness depends less upon our circumstances than upon our thoughts. When we turn our thoughts to God, to his gifts, and to his glorious creation, we experience the joy that God intends for his children. But, when we focus on the negative aspects of life, we suffer needlessly.

The fullness of life in Christ is available to all who seek it and claim it. Count yourself among that number. Seek first the salvation that is available through a personal relationship with Jesus Christ, and then claim the joy, the peace, and the spiritual abundance that the Good Shepherd offers his sheep.

God has charged Himself with full responsibility for our eternal happiness and stands ready to take over the management of our lives the moment we turn in faith to Him.

A. W. TOZER

True happiness consists only in the enjoyment of God. His favor is life, and his loving-kindness is better than life.

ARTHUR W. PINK

Christ is the secret, the source, the substance, the center, and the circumference of all true and lasting gladness.

MRS. CHARLES E. COWMAN

TODAY'S PRAYER

Dear Lord, I am thankful for all the blessings you have given me. Let me be a happy Christian, Father, as I share your joy with friends, with family, and with the world.

Amen.

God's Guidebook

*You will be a good minister of Christ Jesus,
nourished on the truths of the faith and of the good
teaching that you have followed.*

1 Timothy 4:6

God has given us a guidebook for righteous living called the Holy Bible. It contains thorough instructions which, if followed, lead to fulfillment, righteousness, and salvation. But, if we choose to ignore God's commandments, the results are as predictable as they are tragic.

God has given us the Bible for the purpose of knowing his promises, his power, his commandments, his wisdom, his love, and his Son. As we study God's teachings and apply them to our lives, we live by the Word that shall never pass away.

Today, let us follow God's commandments, and let us conduct our lives in such a way that we might be shining examples to our friends, to our families, and, most importantly, to those who have not yet found Christ.

The Bible is the treasure map that leads us to God's highest treasure: eternal life.

MAX LUCADO

The Bible is a Christian's guidebook, and I believe the knowledge it sheds on pain and suffering is the great antidote to fear for suffering people. Knowledge can dissolve fear as light destroys darkness.

PHILIP YANCEY

The Bible is not a guidebook to a theological museum. It is a road map showing us the way into neglected or even forgotten glories of the living God.

RAYMOND ORTLUND

TODAY'S PRAYER

Lord, you've given me instructions for life here on earth and for life eternal. I will use the Bible as my guide. I will study it and meditate upon it as I trust you, Lord, to speak to me through your Holy Word.

Amen.

TOO BUSY?

*The plans of the diligent lead to profit
as surely as haste leads to poverty.*

PROVERBS 21:5

Has the hectic pace of life robbed you of the peace that might otherwise be yours through Jesus Christ? Are you one of those people who is simply too busy for your own good? If so, you're doing a disservice to yourself and your family.

Through his Son Jesus, God offers you a peace that goes beyond human understanding, but he won't force his peace upon you; in order to experience it, you must slow down long enough to sense his presence and his love.

Today, as a gift to yourself, to your family, and to the world, be still and claim the inner peace that is your spiritual birthright—the peace of Jesus Christ. It is offered freely; it has been paid for in full; it is yours for the asking. So ask. And then share.

Often our lives are strangled by things that don't ultimately matter.

GRADY NUTT

In our tense, uptight society where folks are rushing to make appointments they have already missed, a good laugh can be as refreshing as a cup of cold water in the desert.

BARBARA JOHNSON

Being busy, in and of itself, is not a sin. But being busy in an endless pursuit of things that leave us empty and hollow and broken inside—that cannot be pleasing to God.

MAX LUCADO

We often become mentally and spiritually barren because we're so busy.

FRANKLIN GRAHAM

TODAY'S PRAYER

Dear Lord, when the quickening pace of life leaves me with little time for worship or for praise, help me to reorder my priorities, and let me turn to Jesus for the peace that only he can give.

Amen.

Always with Us

For to us a child is born, to us a son is given,
and the government will be on his shoulders.
And he will be called Wonderful Counselor,
Mighty God, Everlasting Father, Prince of Peace.

Isaiah 9:6

A re you facing difficult circumstances or unwelcome changes? If so, please remember that God is far bigger than any problem you may face. So, instead of worrying about life's inevitable challenges, put your faith in the Father and his only begotten Son. "Jesus Christ is the same yesterday and today and forever" (Hebrews 13:8). And remember: It is precisely because your Savior does not change that you can face your challenges with courage for today and hope for tomorrow.

Life is often challenging, but as Christians, we should not be afraid. God loves us, and he will protect us. In times of hardship, he will comfort us; in times of change, he will guide our steps. When we are troubled or weak or sorrowful, God is always with us. We must build our lives on the rock that cannot be moved. We must trust in God. Always.

In a world kept chaotic by change, you will eventually discover, as I have, that this is one of the most precious qualities of the God we are looking for: He doesn't change.

BILL HYBELS

The Holy Spirit can reveal to you why you are stuck, and he can empower you to change (although he won't usually do all the work without your involvement).

PATSY CLAIRMONT

The secret of contentment in the midst of change is found in having roots in the changeless Christ—the same yesterday, today and forever.

ED YOUNG

TODAY'S PRAYER

Dear Lord, our world is constantly changing. When I face the inevitable transitions of life, I will turn to you for strength and assurance. Thank you, Father, for love that is unchanging and everlasting.

Amen.

Relying upon Him

Humble yourselves, therefore, under God's mighty hand, that he may lift you up in due time. Cast all your anxiety on him because he cares for you.

1 Peter 5:6-7

Do the demands of this day threaten to overwhelm you? If so, you must rely not only upon your own resources but also upon the promises of your Father in heaven.

God is a never-ending source of support and courage for those of us who call upon him. When we are weary, he gives us strength. When we see no hope, God reminds us of his promises. When we grieve, God wipes away our tears.

God will hold your hand and walk with you every day of your life if you let him. So even if your circumstances are difficult, trust the Father. His love is eternal, and his goodness endures forever.

Faith is not merely you holding on to God—it is God holding on to you.

E. Stanley Jones

When you have no helpers, see all your helpers in God. When you have many helpers, see God in all your helpers. When you have nothing but God, see all in God; when you have everything, see God in everything. Under all conditions, stay thy heart only on the Lord.

C. H. SPURGEON

The more you give your mental burdens to the Lord, the more exciting it becomes to see how God will handle things that are impossible for you to do anything about.

CHARLES SWINDOLL

God uses our most stumbling, faltering faith-steps as the open door to His doing for us "more than we ask or think."

CATHERINE MARSHALL

TODAY'S PRAYER

Heavenly Father, you never leave or forsake me. You are always with me, protecting me and encouraging me. Whatever this day may bring, I thank you for your love and your strength.

Amen.

Growing in Christ

*When I was a child, I talked like a child, I thought
like a child, I reasoned like a child. When I became
a man, I put the ways of childhood behind me.*

1 Corinthians 13:11

The journey toward spiritual maturity lasts a lifetime. As Christians, we can and should continue to grow in the love and the knowledge of our Savior as long as we live.

When we cease to grow, either emotionally or spiritually, we do ourselves a profound disservice. But, if we study God's Word, if we obey his commandments, and if we live in the center of his will, we will not be stagnant believers; we will, instead, be growing Christians. And that's exactly what God wants for our lives.

With God, it isn't who you were that matters; it's who you are becoming.

LIZ CURTIS HIGGS

The instrument of our sanctification is the Word of God. The Spirit of God brings to our minds the precepts and doctrines of truth, and applies them with power. The truth is our sanctifier. If we do not hear or read it, we will not grow in sanctification.

C. H. Spurgeon

The process of growing up is to me valued for what we gain, not for what we lose.

C. S. Lewis

Today's Prayer

Dear Lord, I know that I still have so many things to learn. I won't stop learning, I won't give up, and I won't stop growing. Every day, I will do my best to become a little bit more like the person you intend for me to be.

Amen.

Honoring God

Honor the LORD with your wealth,
with the firstfruits of all your crops;
then your barns will be filled to overflowing,
and your vats will brim over with new wine.

PROVERBS 3:9–10

At times, your life is probably hectic, demanding, and complicated. When the demands of life leave you rushing from place to place with scarcely a moment to spare, you may fail to pause and thank your Creator for the blessings he has bestowed upon you. But that's a big mistake.

Whom will you choose to honor today? If you honor God and place him at the center of your life, every day is a cause for celebration. But if you fail to honor your heavenly Father, you're asking for trouble, and lots of it.

So honor God for who he is and for what he has done for you. And don't just honor him on Sunday morning. Praise him all day long, every day, for as long as you live—and then for all eternity.

God shows unbridled delight when He sees people acting in ways that honor Him.

BILL HYBELS

We honor God by asking for great things when they are a part of His promise. We dishonor Him and cheat ourselves when we ask for molehills where He has promised mountains.

VANCE HAVNER

Happiness is to be found only in the home where God is loved and honored, where each one loves, and helps, and cares for the others.

ST. THEOPHANE VENARD

TODAY'S PRAYER

I praise you, Lord, from the depths of my heart,
and I give thanks for your goodness, for your mercy,
and for your Son. Let me honor you every day
of my life through my words and my deeds.
Let me honor you, Father, with all that I am.

Amen.

BEYOND GUILT

There is now no condemnation
for those who are in Christ Jesus.

ROMANS 8:1

All of us have sinned. Sometimes our sins result from our own stubborn rebellion against God's commandments. And sometimes, we are swept up in events that are beyond our abilities to control. Under either set of circumstances, we may experience intense feelings of guilt.

But God has an answer for the guilt that we feel. That answer, of course, is his forgiveness. When we confess our wrongdoings, and repent from them, we are forgiven by the One who created us.

Are you troubled by feelings of guilt or regret? If so, you must repent from your misdeeds, and you must ask your heavenly Father for his forgiveness. When you do so, he will forgive you completely and without reservation. Then, you must forgive yourself just as God has forgiven you—thoroughly and unconditionally.

Prayer is essential when a believer is stuck in the pits of unresolved guilt.

CHARLES STANLEY

Let's take Jesus at his word. When he says we're forgiven, let's unload the guilt. When he says we're valuable, let's believe him. When he says we're eternal, let's bury our fear. When he says we're provided for, let's stop worrying.

MAX LUCADO

Spiritual life without guilt would be like physical life without pain. Guilt is a defense mechanism; it's like an alarm that goes off to lead you to confession when you sin.

JOHN MACARTHUR

TODAY'S PRAYER

Dear Lord, thank you for the guilt that I feel when I disobey you. Help me confess my wrongdoings, help me accept your forgiveness, and help me renew my passion to serve you.

Amen.

WE BELONG TO HIM

Return to the LORD your God, for he is gracious and
compassionate, slow to anger and abounding in love,
and he relents from sending calamity.

JOEL 2:13

The line from the children's song is reassuring and familiar: "Little ones to him belong. We are weak but he is strong." That message applies to kids of all ages. We are all indeed weak, but we worship a mighty God who meets our needs and answers our prayers.

Are you in the midst of adversity or in the grips of temptation? If so, turn to God for strength. The Bible promises that you can do all things through the power of our risen Savior, Jesus Christ. Your challenge, then, is clear: You must place Christ where he belongs—at the very center of your life. When you do, you will discover that, yes, Jesus loves you and that, yes, he will give you direction and strength if you ask it in his name.

Our hearts have been made to cry out for a love that can come only from our Creator.

ANGELA THOMAS

God knows all that is true about us and is a friend to the face we show and the face we hide. He does not love us less for our human weaknesses.

SHEILA WALSH

God loves me as God loves all people, without qualification. To be in the image of God means that all of us are made for the purpose of knowing and loving God and one another and of being loved in turn, not literally in the same way God knows and loves, but in a way appropriate to human beings.

ROBERTA BONDI

TODAY'S PRAYER

Thank you, Lord, for your love.
Your love is boundless, infinite, and eternal. Today, as I pause and reflect upon your love for me, let me share that love with all those who cross my path. And, as an expression of my love for you, Father, let me share the saving message of your Son with a world in desperate need of his hope, his peace, and his salvation.

Amen.

HE IS HERE

*Where can I go from your Spirit? Where can I flee
from your presence? If I go up to the heavens, you are
there; if I make my bed in the depths, you are there.
If I rise on the wings of the dawn, if I settle on the far
side of the sea, even there your hand will guide me,
your right hand will hold me fast.*

PSALM 139:7-10

If God is everywhere, why does he sometimes seem so far away? The answer to that question, of course, has nothing to do with God and everything to do with us.

When we begin each day on our knees, in praise and worship to him, God often seems very near indeed. But, if we ignore God's presence or—worse yet—rebel against it altogether, the world in which we live becomes a spiritual wasteland.

Today and every day, thank God and praise him. He is the giver of all things good. Wherever you are, whether you are happy or sad, victorious or vanquished, celebrate God's presence. And be comforted. For he is here.

If your heart has grown cold, it is because you have moved away from the fire of His presence.

BETH MOORE

God walks with us. He scoops us up in His arms or simply sits with us in silent strength until we cannot avoid the awesome recognition that yes, even now, He is here.

GLORIA GAITHER

Certainly, God is with us in times of distress, and that is a comforting truth. But listen: Jesus wants to be part of every experience and every moment of our lives.

BILLY GRAHAM

We may ignore, but we can nowhere evade, the presence of God. The world is crowded with Him. He walks everywhere incognito. And the incognito is not always hard to penetrate. The real labour is to remember, to attend. In fact, to come awake. Still more, to remain awake.

C. S. LEWIS

TODAY'S PRAYER

Heavenly Father, even when it seems to me that you are far away, you never leave my side. Today and every day, I will strive to feel your presence, and I will strive to sense your love for me.

Amen.

The Lessons of Tough Times

I waited patiently for the LORD; he turned to me and heard my cry. He lifted me out of the slimy pit, out of the mud and mire; he set my feet on a rock and gave me a firm place to stand. He put a new song in my mouth, a hymn of praise to our God.

PSALM 40:1-3

Life can be difficult at times. And everybody makes mistakes. Your job is to make them only once.

Have you experienced a recent setback? If so, look for the lesson that God is trying to teach you. Instead of complaining about life's sad state of affairs, learn what needs to be learned, change what needs to be changed, and move on. View failure as an opportunity to reassess God's will for your life. View life's inevitable disappointments as opportunities to learn more about yourself and your world.

No matter what trials we face, Christ never leaves us.

BILLY GRAHAM

God is able to take mistakes, when they are committed to Him, and make of them something for our good and for His glory.

RUTH BELL GRAHAM

Father, take our mistakes and turn them into opportunities.

MAX LUCADO

TODAY'S PRAYER

Lord, I know that I am imperfect and that I fail you in many ways. Thank you for your forgiveness and for your unconditional love. Show me the error of my ways, Lord, that I might confess my wrongdoing and correct my mistakes. And, let me grow each day in wisdom, in faith, and in my love for you.

Amen.

GIVE ME PATIENCE, LORD, RIGHT NOW!

We urge you, brothers and sisters,
warn those who are idle and disruptive,
encourage the disheartened,
help the weak, be patient with everyone.

1 THESSALONIANS 5:14

As busy people living in a fast-paced world, many of us find that waiting quietly for God is difficult. Most of us are impatient for God to grant us the desires of our heart. Usually, we know what we want, and we know precisely when we want it—right now, if not sooner. But God may have other plans. And when God's plans differ from our own, we must trust in his infinite wisdom and in his infinite love.

God instructs us to be patient in all things. We must be patient with our families, our friends, and our associates. We must also be patient with our Creator as he unfolds his plan for our lives. And that's as it should be. After all, think how patient God has been with us.

Two signposts of faith: "Slow Down" and "Wait Here."

CHARLES STANLEY

Our challenge is to wait in faith for the day of God's favor and salvation.

JIM CYMBALA

How do you wait upon the Lord? First you must learn to sit at His feet and take time to listen to His words.

KAY ARTHUR

As we wait on God, He helps us use the winds of adversity to soar above our problems. As the Bible says, "Those who wait on the LORD . . . shall mount up with wings like eagles."

BILLY GRAHAM

TODAY'S PRAYER

Dear Lord, let me live according to your plan and according to your timetable. When I am hurried, Lord, slow me down. When I become impatient with others, give me empathy. Today, Lord, let me be a patient Christian, and let me trust in you and in your master plan.

Amen.

THE WORLD'S BEST FRIEND

Greater love has no one than this:
to lay down one's life for one's friends.

JOHN 15:13

Who's the best friend this world has ever had? Jesus, of course! When you invite him to become Lord of your life, Jesus will be your friend, too . . . your friend forever.

Jesus has offered to share the gifts of everlasting life and everlasting love with the world . . . and with you. If you make mistakes, he'll still be your friend. If you behave badly, he'll still love you. If you feel sorry or sad, he can help you feel better.

Jesus wants you to have a happy, healthy life. He wants you to be generous and kind. He wants you to follow his example. And the rest is up to you. You can do it! And with a friend like Jesus, you will.

What a friend we have in Jesus, all our sins and griefs to bear! What a privilege to carry everything to God in prayer! O what peace we often forfeit, O what needless pain we bear, all because we do not carry everything to God in prayer. Have we trials and temptations? Is there trouble anywhere? We should never be discouraged;

take it to the Lord in prayer. Can we find a friend so faithful who will all our sorrows share? Jesus knows our every weakness; take it to the Lord in prayer. Are we weak and heavy laden, cumbered with a load of care? Precious Savior, still our refuge; take it to the Lord in prayer. Do thy friends despise, forsake thee? Take it to the Lord in prayer! In his arms he'll take and shield thee; thou wilt find a solace there.

JOSEPH M. SCRIVEN

The dearest friend on earth is but a mere shadow compared with Jesus Christ.

OSWALD CHAMBERS

In the Gospels the Lord Jesus is presented as the Friend of sinners, for historically He was found, first of all, moving among the people as their Friend before He became their Savior. But do you realize that today He is still in the first place our Friend, in order that He might become our Savior?

WATCHMAN NEE

TODAY'S PRAYER

Dear Jesus, you are my Savior and my protector. Give me the courage to trust you completely. Today, I will praise you, I will honor you, and I will live according to your commandments. Amen.

A Godly Leader

The noble make noble plans,
and by noble deeds they stand.

ISAIAH 32:8

Our world needs Christian leaders who willingly honor God with their words and their deeds, but not necessarily in that order.

If you seek to be a godly leader, then you must begin by being a worthy example to your family, to your friends, to your church, and to your community. After all, your words of instruction will never ring true unless you yourself are willing to follow them.

Are you the kind of leader whom you would want to follow? If so, congratulations. But if the answer to that question is no, then it's time to improve your leadership skills, beginning with the words that you speak and the example that you set, but not necessarily in that order.

The goal of leadership is to empower the whole people of God to discern and to discharge the Lord's will.

STANLEY GRENZ

A true and safe leader is likely to be one who has no desire to lead, but is forced into a position of leadership by inward pressure of the Holy Spirit and the press of external situation.

A. W. TOZER

The man who kneels before God will stand before men.

LEONARD RAVENHILL

TODAY'S PRAYER

Dear Lord, when I find myself in a position of leadership, let me seek your will and obey your commandments. Let me be a Christ-centered leader, and let me turn to you, Father, for guidance, for courage, for wisdom, and for love.

Amen.

THE WISDOM OF MODERATION

Better a patient person than a warrior,
one with self-control than one who takes a city.

PROVERBS 16:32

Moderation and wisdom are traveling companions. If we are wise, we must learn to temper our appetites, our desires, and our impulses. When we do, we are blessed, in part, because God has created a world in which temperance is rewarded and intemperance is inevitably punished.

Would you like to improve your life? Then harness your appetites and restrain your impulses. Moderation is difficult, of course; it is especially difficult in a prosperous society such as ours. But the rewards of moderation are numerous and long-lasting. Claim those rewards today. No one can force you to moderate your appetites. The decision to live temperately (and wisely) is yours and yours alone. And so are the consequences.

Every moment of resistance to temptation is a victory.

FREDERICK WILLIAM FABER

We are all created differently. We share a common need to balance the different parts of our lives.

DR. WALT LARIMORE

Virtue—even attempted virtue—brings light; indulgence brings fog.

C. S. LEWIS

TODAY'S PRAYER

Dear Lord, give me the wisdom to be moderate and self-disciplined. Let me strive to do your will here on earth, and as I do, let me find contentment and balance. Let me be a disciplined believer, Father, today and every day.

Amen.

Look Up and Move On

Get rid of all bitterness, rage and anger, brawling and slander, along with every form of malice. Be kind and compassionate to one another, forgiving each other, just as in Christ God forgave you.

EPHESIANS 4:31-32

The world holds few if any rewards for those who remain angrily focused upon the past. Still, the act of forgiveness is difficult for all but the saintliest men and women. Are you mired in the quicksand of bitterness or regret? If so, you are not only disobeying God's Word, you are also wasting your time.

Being frail, fallible, imperfect human beings, most of us are quick to anger, quick to blame, slow to forgive, and even slower to forget. Yet as Christians, we are commanded to forgive others, just as we, too, have been forgiven.

If there exists even one person—alive or dead—against whom you hold bitter feelings, it's time to forgive. Or, if you are embittered against yourself for some past mistake or shortcoming, it's finally time to forgive yourself and move on. Hatred, bitterness, and regret are not part of God's plan for your life. Forgiveness is.

Be so preoccupied with good will that you haven't room for ill will.

E. STANLEY JONES

Acrid bitterness inevitably seeps into the lives of people who harbor grudges and suppress anger, and bitterness is always a poison.

LEE STROBEL

Anger breeds remorse in the heart, discord in the home, bitterness in the community, and confusion in the state.

BILLY GRAHAM

Grudges are like hand grenades; It is wise to release them before they destroy you.

BARBARA JOHNSON

TODAY'S PRAYER

Heavenly Father, free me from anger and bitterness. When I am angry, I cannot feel the peace that you intend for my life. When I am bitter, I cannot sense your presence. Keep me mindful that forgiveness is your commandment. Let me turn away from bitterness and instead claim the spiritual abundance that you offer through the gift of your Son. Amen.

THE VOICE INSIDE YOUR HEAD

I strive always to keep my conscience clear before God and man.

ACTS 24:16

Your conscience is an early-warning system designed to keep you out of trouble. When you're about to do something that you know is wrong, a little voice inside your head has a way of speaking up. If you listen to that voice, you'll be okay; if you ignore it, you're asking for headaches or heartbreaks—or both.

Whenever you're about to make an important decision, you should listen carefully to the quiet voice inside. Sometimes, of course, it's tempting to do otherwise. From time to time you'll be tempted to abandon your better judgement by ignoring your conscience. But remember that a conscience is a terrible thing to waste.

So instead of ignoring that quiet little voice, pay careful attention to it. If you do, your conscience will lead you in the right direction—in fact, it's trying to lead you right now. So listen . . . and learn.

Your conscience is your alarm system. It's your protection.

CHARLES STANLEY

God desires that we become spiritually healthy enough through faith to have a conscience that rightly interprets the work of the Holy Spirit.

BETH MOORE

You should not believe your conscience and your feelings more than the word which the Lord who receives sinners preaches to you.

MARTIN LUTHER

The beginning of backsliding means your conscience does not answer to the truth.

OSWALD SANDERS

TODAY'S PRAYER

Dear God, you've given me a conscience that tells me right from wrong. Let me trust my conscience, and let me live according to your teachings, not just for today, but forever.

Amen.

ENCOURAGING WORDS FOR FAMILY AND FRIENDS

Do not let any unwholesome talk come out of your mouths, but only what is helpful for building others up according to their needs, that it may benefit those who listen.

EPHESIANS 4:29

Life is a team sport, and all of us need occasional pats on the back from our teammates. As Christians, we are called upon to spread the good news of Christ, and we are also called to spread a message of encouragement and hope to the world.

Whether you realize it or not, many people with whom you come in contact every day are in desperate need of a smile or an encouraging word. The world can be a difficult place, and countless friends and family members may be troubled by the challenges of everyday life.

Since you don't always know who needs our help, the best strategy is to try to encourage all the people who cross your path. So today, be a world-class source of encouragement to everyone you meet. Never has the need been greater.

We do have the ability to encourage or discourage each other with the words we say. In order to maintain a positive mood, our hearts must be in good condition.

ANNIE CHAPMAN

Encouraging others means helping people, looking for the best in them, and trying to bring out their positive qualities.

JOHN MAXWELL

To the loved, a word of affection is a morsel, but to the love-starved, a word of affection can be a feast.

MAX LUCADO

TODAY'S PRAYER

Dear heavenly Father, because I am your child,
I am blessed. You have loved me eternally,
cared for me faithfully, and saved me through
the gift of your Son, Jesus. Just as you have lifted
me up, Lord, let me lift up others in a spirit of
encouragement and optimism and hope.
And, if I can help a fellow traveler, even in a small
way, dear Lord, may the glory be yours.

Amen.

Your Traveling Companion

Thanks be to God! He gives us the victory through our Lord Jesus Christ. Therefore, my dear brothers and sisters, stand firm. Let nothing move you. Always give yourselves fully to the work of the Lord, because you know that your labor in the Lord is not in vain.

1 Corinthians 15:57–58

As you continue to seek God's purpose for your life, you will undoubtedly experience your fair share of disappointments, detours, false starts, and failures. When you do, don't become discouraged. God's not finished with you yet.

The old saying is as true today as it was when it was first spoken: "Life is a marathon, not a sprint." That's why wise travelers select a traveling companion who never tires and never falters. That partner, of course, is your heavenly Father. So pray as if everything depended upon God, and work as if everything depended upon you. And trust God to do the rest.

By perseverance the snail reached the ark.

C. H. Spurgeon

Failure is one of life's most powerful teachers. How we handle our failures determines whether we're going to simply "get by" in life or "press on."

Beth Moore

If things are tough, remember that every flower that ever bloomed had to go through a whole lot of dirt to get there.

Barbara Johnson

Today's Prayer

Dear Lord, when I want to give up, help me remember how important it is to keep trying. And when I'm worried or upset, help me remember to talk to my family and to you.

Amen.

LIFE ETERNAL

Because I live, you also will live.

JOHN 14:19

Ours is not a distant God. Ours is a God who understands—far better than we ever could—the essence of what it means to be human. How marvelous it is that God became a man and walked among us. Had he not chosen to do so, we might feel removed from a distant Creator.

God understands our hopes, our fears, and our temptations. He understands what it means to be angry and what it costs to forgive. He knows the heart, the conscience, and the soul of every person who has ever lived, including you. And God has a plan of salvation that is intended for you. Accept it. Accept God's gift through the person of his Son, Christ Jesus, and then rest assured. God walked among us so that you might have eternal life; amazing though it may seem, he did it for you.

The gift of God is eternal life, spiritual life, abundant life through faith in Jesus Christ, the Living Word of God.

ANNE GRAHAM LOTZ

Teach us to set our hopes on heaven, to hold firmly to the promise of eternal life, so that we can withstand the struggles and storms of this world.

MAX LUCADO

How completely satisfying to turn from our limitations to a God who has none. Eternal years lie in his heart. For him time does not pass, it remains; and those who are in Christ share with him all the riches of limitless time and endless years.

A. W. TOZER

TODAY'S PRAYER

I know, Lord, that this world is not my home;
I am only here for a brief while.
And you have given me the priceless gift of eternal life through your Son, Jesus. Keep the hope of heaven fresh in my heart, and, while I am in this world, help me to pass through it with faith in my heart and praise on my lips—praise for you.

Amen.

FORGIVE: IT'S GOD'S WAY

Be kind and compassionate to one another,
forgiving each other, just as in Christ God forgave you.

EPHESIANS 4:32

Forgiveness, no matter how difficult, is God's way, and it must be our way, too. To forgive others is difficult. Being frail, fallible, imperfect human beings, we are quick to anger, quick to blame, slow to forgive, and even slower to forget. No matter.

God's commandments are not intended to be customized for the particular whims of particular believers. God's Word is not a menu from which each of us may select items à la carte, according to our own desires. Far from it. God's Holy Word is a book that must be taken in its entirety; all of God's commandments are to be taken seriously.

And, so it is with forgiveness. So, if you hold bitterness against even a single person, forgive. Then, to the best of your abilities, forget. It's God's way for you to live.

God expects us to forgive others as He has forgiven us; we are to follow His example by having a forgiving heart.

VONETTE BRIGHT

Learning how to forgive and forget is one of the secrets of a happy Christian life.

WARREN WIERSBE

I believe that forgiveness can become a continuing cycle: because God forgives us, we're to forgive others; because we forgive others, God forgives us. Scripture presents both parts of the cycle.

SHIRLEY DOBSON

TODAY'S PRAYER

Heavenly Father, genuine forgiveness is difficult. Help me to forgive those who have injured me, and deliver me from the traps of anger and bitterness. Forgiveness is your way, Lord; let it be mine.

Amen.

NEIGHBORS IN NEED

*Each of us should please our neighbors
for their good, to build them up.[3]
For even Christ did not please himself.*

ROMANS 15:2–3

Neighbors. We know that we are instructed to love them, and yet there's so little time . . . and we're so busy. No matter. As Christians, we are commanded by our Lord and Savior Jesus Christ to love our neighbors just as we love ourselves. Period.

This very day, you will encounter someone who needs a word of encouragement, a pat on the back, a helping hand, or a heartfelt prayer.

- If you don't reach out to your friend, who will?

- If you don't take the time to understand the needs of your neighbors, who will?

- If you don't love your brothers and sisters, who will?

So, today, look for a neighbor in need . . . and then do something to help. Father's orders.

The truest help we can render an afflicted man is not to take his burden from him, but to call out his best energy, that he may be able to bear the burden himself.

PHILLIPS BROOKS

Make it a rule, and pray to God to help you to keep it, never, if possible, to lie down at night without being able to say: "I have made one human being at least a little wiser, or a little happier, or at least a little better this day."

CHARLES KINGSLEY

Do all the good you can. By all the means you can. In all the ways you can. In all the places you can. At all the times you can. To all the people you can. As long as ever you can.

JOHN WESLEY

TODAY'S PRAYER

Heavenly Father, help me be a Good Samaritan
to the people you place along my path,
today and every day.

Amen.

Your Real Riches

Naked I came from my mother's womb, and naked I will depart. The LORD gave and the LORD has taken away; may the name of the LORD be praised.

JOB 1:21

Earthly riches are transitory; spiritual riches are not. Martin Luther observed, "Many things I have tried to grasp and have lost. That which I have placed in God's hands I still have." How true.

In our demanding world, financial security can be a good thing, but spiritual prosperity is profoundly more important. Certainly we all need the basic necessities of life, but once we've acquired those necessities, enough is enough.

Why? Because our real riches are not of this world. We are never really rich until we are rich in spirit.

He is no fool who gives what he cannot keep to gain what he cannot lose.

JIM ELLIOT

Wealth is something entrusted to us by God, something God doesn't want us to trust. He wants us to trust Him.

WARREN WIERSBE

When possessions become our god, we become materialistic and greedy . . . and we forfeit our contentment and our joy.

CHARLES SWINDOLL

What we possess often possesses us—we are possessed by possessions.

OSWALD CHAMBERS

TODAY'S PRAYER

Dear Lord, all I have belongs to you. When I leave this world, I take nothing with me. Help me to value my relationship with you—and my relationships with others—more than I value my material possessions.

Amen.

REAL REPENTANCE

*I preached that they should repent and turn to God
and demonstrate their repentance by their deeds.*

ACTS 26:20

Who among us has sinned? All of us. But the good news is this: When we do ask God's forgiveness and turn our hearts to him, he forgives us absolutely and completely.

Genuine repentance requires more than simply offering God apologies for our misdeeds. Real repentance may start with feelings of sorrow and remorse, but it ends only when we turn away from the sin that has distanced us from our Creator.

In truth, we offer our most meaningful apologies to God, not with our words, but with our actions. As long as we are still engaged in sin, we may be *repenting*, but we have not fully *repented*. So, if there is an aspect of your life that is distancing you from your God, ask for his forgiveness, and—just as importantly—stop sinning. Now.

Repentance is the first conscious movement of the soul away from sin and toward God.

SAM JONES

Repentance involves a radical change of heart and mind in which we agree with God's evaluation of our sin and then take specific action to align ourselves with His will.

HENRY BLACKABY

True repentance is admitting that what God says is true, and that because it is true, we change our minds about our sins and about the Savior.

WARREN WIERSBE

Repentance becomes a way of life, a lifelong process of turning towards the Holy One, that happens one day at a time.

TREVOR HUDSON

TODAY'S PRAYER

When I stray from your commandments, Lord, I must not only confess my sins, I must also turn from them. When I fall short, help me to change. Forgive my sins, dear Lord, and help me live according to your plan for my life. Your plan is perfect, Father; I am not. Let me trust in you.

Amen.

CONQUERING EVERYDAY FRUSTRATIONS

A hot-tempered person stirs up conflict,
but the one who is patient calms a quarrel.

PROVERBS 15:18

L ife is full of frustrations—some great and some small. On occasion, you, like Jesus, will confront evil, and when you do, you may respond as he did—vigorously and without reservation.

But, more often your frustrations will be of the more mundane variety. As long as you live here on earth, you will face countless opportunities to lose your temper over small, relatively insignificant events: a traffic jam, a spilled cup of coffee, an inconsiderate comment, a broken promise.

When you are tempted to lose your temper over the minor inconveniences of life, don't. Turn away from anger, hatred, bitterness, and regret. Turn instead to God. When you do, you'll be following his commandments and giving yourself a priceless gift . . . the gift of peace.

Frustration is not the will of God. There is time to do anything and everything that God wants us to do.

ELISABETH ELLIOT

Anger is the noise of the soul; the unseen irritant of the heart; the relentless invader of silence.

MAX LUCADO

We must lay our questions, frustrations, anxieties, and impotence at the feet of God and wait for His answer. And then receiving it, we must live by faith.

KAY ARTHUR

TODAY'S PRAYER

Dear Lord, when I am angry, I cannot feel the peace that you intend for my life. When I am bitter, I cannot sense your love. Heavenly Father, keep me mindful that forgiveness is your commandment and your will for my life. Let me turn away from anger and instead claim the spiritual abundance that you offer through the priceless gift of your Son, Jesus.

Amen.

GOD'S TIMETABLE

Humble yourselves, therefore, under God's mighty hand, that he may lift you up in due time.

1 PETER 5:6

Sometimes, the hardest thing to do is to wait. This is especially true when we're in a hurry and when we want things to happen now, if not sooner! But God's plan does not always happen in the way that we would like or at the time of our own choosing. Our task—as believing Christians who trust in a benevolent, all-knowing Father—is to wait patiently for God to reveal himself.

We human beings are, by nature, impatient. We know what we want, and we know exactly when we want it—RIGHT NOW! But, God knows better. He has created a world that unfolds according to his own timetable, not ours. Thank goodness!

Waiting on God brings us to the journey's end quicker than our feet.

MRS. CHARLES E. COWMAN

Will not the Lord's time be better than your time?

C. H. Spurgeon

God is not hurried along in the Time-stream of this universe any more than an author is hurried along in the imaginary time of his own novel. He has infinite attention to spare for each one of us. He does not have to deal with us in the mass. You are as much alone with Him as if you were the only being He had ever created. When Christ died, He died for you individually just as much as if you have been the only man in the world.

C. S. Lewis

Today's Prayer

Dear Lord, your timing is always right for me.
You have a plan for my life that is grander than I
can imagine. When I am impatient, remind me that
you are never early or late. You are always on time,
Father, so let me trust in you . . . always.

Amen.

Roadmap for Life

*Every word of God is flawless;
he is a shield to those who take refuge in him.*

PROVERBS 30:5

God's Word is a roadmap for life here on earth and for life eternal. As Christians, we are called upon to study God's Holy Word, to trust its promises, to follow its commandments, and to share its good news with the world.

As believers, we must study the Bible and meditate upon its meaning for our lives. Otherwise, we deprive ourselves of a priceless gift from our Creator. God's Holy Word is, indeed, a transforming, life-changing, one-of-a-kind treasure. And, a passing acquaintance with the Good Book is insufficient for Christians who seek to obey God's Word and to understand his will. After all, neither man nor woman should live by bread alone . . .

Walking in faith brings you to the Word of God. There you will be healed, cleansed, fed, nurtured, equipped, and matured.

KAY ARTHUR

God did not write a book and send it by messenger to be read at a distance by unaided minds. He spoke a Book and lives in His spoken words, constantly speaking His words and causing the power of them to persist across the years.

A. W. Tozer

The only way we can understand the Bible is by personal contact with the Living Word.

Oswald Chambers

There is no way to draw closer to God unless you are in the Word of God every day. It's your compass. Your guide. You can't get where you need to go without it.

Stormie Omartian

Today's Prayer

Heavenly Father, your Holy Word is a light unto my path. In all that I do, help me be a worthy witness for you as I share the good news of your perfect Son and your perfect Word.

Amen.

ACTIONS THAT REFLECT OUR BELIEFS

Everything that does not come from faith is sin.

ROMANS 14:23

Are you the kind of practical Christian who is willing to dig in and do what needs to be done when it needs to be done? If so, congratulations! God acknowledges your service and blesses it. But if you find yourself more interested in the fine points of theology than in the needs of your neighbors, it's time to rearrange your priorities.

As Christians, we must do our best to ensure that our actions are accurate reflections of our beliefs. Our theology must be demonstrated, not only by our words but, more importantly, by our actions. In short, we should be practical believers, quick to act whenever we see an opportunity to serve God.

God needs believers who are willing to roll up their sleeves and go to work for him. Count yourself among that number. Theology is a good thing unless it interferes with God's work. And it's up to you to make certain that your theology doesn't.

Do noble things, do not dream them all day long.

CHARLES KINGSLEY

Although our actions have nothing to do with gaining our own salvation, they might be used by God to save somebody else! What we do really matters, and it can affect the eternities of people we care about.

BILL HYBELS

Let us not be content to wait and see what will happen, but give us the determination to make the right things happen.

PETER MARSHALL

TODAY'S PRAYER

Heavenly Father, I believe in you,
and I believe in your Word. Help me to live
in such a way that my actions validate my beliefs—
and let the glory be yours forever.

Amen.

THE RIGHT KIND OF BEHAVIOR

*We know that we have come to know him
if we keep his commands.*

1 JOHN 2:3

When we behave ourselves as godly men, we honor God. When we live righteously and according to God's commandments, he blesses us in ways that we cannot fully understand. When we seek righteousness in our own lives—and when we seek the companionship of those who do likewise—we reap the spiritual rewards that God intends for us to enjoy.

Today, as you fulfill your responsibilities, hold fast to that which is good, and associate yourself with believers who behave themselves in like fashion. When you do, your good works will serve as a powerful example for others and as a worthy offering to your Creator.

A pure theology and a loose morality will never mix.

C. H. SPURGEON

Christians are the citizens of heaven, and while we are on earth, we ought to behave like heaven's citizens.

WARREN WIERSBE

Be such a man, and live such a life, that if every man were such as you, and every life a life like yours, this earth would be God's Paradise.

PHILLIPS BROOKS

We should live in light of being called out of this world at any time into the presence of God, where we will receive our eternal reward.

JOHN MACARTHUR

TODAY'S PRAYER

Dear Lord, this world has countless temptations, distractions, interruptions, and frustrations. When I allow my focus to drift away from you and your Word, I suffer. But, when I turn my thoughts and my prayers to you, heavenly Father, you guide my path. Let me discover the right thing to do— and let me do it—this day and every day that I live.

Amen.

HIS RULE, YOUR RULE

*In everything, do to others what you would
have them do to you, for this sums up
the Law and the Prophets.*

MATTHEW 7:12

Is the Golden Rule your rule? Hopefully so. After all, Jesus instructs you to treat other people in the same way that you want to be treated. But sometimes, especially when you're feeling the pressures of everyday living, obeying the Golden Rule can seem like an impossible task—but it's not.

Would you like to make the world a better place? If so, you can start by practicing the Golden Rule. If you want to know how to treat other people, ask the person you see every time you look into the mirror. The answer you receive will tell you exactly what to do.

It is wrong for anyone to be anxious to receive more from his neighbor than he himself is willing to give to God.

ST. FRANCIS OF ASSISI

It is my calling to treat every human being with grace and dignity, to treat every person, whether encountered in a palace or a gas station, as a life made in the image of God.

SHEILA WALSH

It is one of the most beautiful compensations of life that no one can sincerely try to help another without helping herself.

BARBARA JOHNSON

TODAY'S PRAYER

Lord, I thank you for friends and family members who practice the Golden Rule. Because I expect to be treated with kindness, let me be kind. Because I wish to be loved, let me be loving. In all things, Lord, let me live by the Golden Rule, and let me express my gratitude to those who offer kindness to me.

Amen.

Enthusiasm for Christ

With minds that are alert and fully sober,
set your hope on the grace to be brought to you
when Jesus Christ is revealed at his coming.
As obedient children, do not conform to the evil
desires you had when you lived in ignorance.
But just as he who called you is holy,
so be holy in all you do.

1 Peter 1:13–15

When we fan the flames of enthusiasm for Christ, our faith serves as a beacon to others. John Wesley advised, "Catch on fire with enthusiasm and people will come for miles to watch you burn." His words still ring true.

Our world desperately needs faithful believers who share the good news of Jesus with joyful exuberance. Be such an enthusiastic believer. The world desperately needs your enthusiasm—now!

Enthusiasm, like the flu, is contagious—we get it from one another.

Barbara Johnson

We act as though comfort and luxury were the chief requirements of life, when all we need to make us really happy is something to be enthusiastic about.

CHARLES KINGSLEY

One of the great needs in the church today is for every Christian to become enthusiastic about his faith in Jesus Christ.

BILLY GRAHAM

Diligence applies to whatever you do in your Christian life. Anything done in the Lord's service is worth doing with enthusiasm and care.

JOHN MACARTHUR

TODAY'S PRAYER

Dear Lord, let me be an enthusiastic participant in life. And let my enthusiasm bring honor and glory to you.

Amen.

Outgrowing Bad Habits

Do not be misled:
"Bad company corrupts good character."

1 Corinthians 15:33

It's an old saying and a true one: First, you make your habits, and then your habits make you. Some habits will inevitably bring you closer to God; other habits will lead you away from the path he has chosen for you. If you sincerely desire to improve your spiritual health, you must honestly examine the habits that make up the fabric of your day. And you must abandon those habits that are displeasing to God.

If you trust God, and if you keep asking for his help, he can transform your life. If you sincerely ask him to help you, the same God who created the universe will help you defeat the harmful habits that have been defeating you. So, if at first you don't succeed, keep praying. God is listening, and he's ready to help you become a better person if you ask him. So ask today.

You will never change your life until you change something you do daily.

JOHN MAXWELL

Since behaviors become habits, make them work with you and not against you.

E. STANLEY JONES

Just as iron, even without willing it, is drawn by a magnet, so is a slave to bad habits dragged about by them.

JOHN CLIMACUS

Do nothing that you would not like to be doing when Jesus comes. Go no place where you would not like to be found when He returns.

CORRIE TEN BOOM

TODAY'S PRAYER

Dear Lord, help me break bad habits and form good ones. And let me make a habit of sharing the things that I own and the love that I feel in my heart.

Amen.

He Overcomes

I have told you these things, so that in me you may
have peace. In this world you will have trouble.
But take heart! I have overcome the world.

John 16:33

There are few sadder sights on earth than the sight of a person who has lost all hope. In difficult times, hope can be elusive, but Christians need never lose it. After all, God is good; his love endures; he has promised his children the gift of eternal life.

If you find yourself falling into the spiritual traps of worry and discouragement, consider the words of Jesus. It was Christ who promised, "I have overcome the world" (John 16:33). This world is indeed a place of trials and tribulations, but as believers, we are secure. God has promised us peace, joy, and eternal life. And, of course, God always keeps his promises.

When you say a situation or a person is hopeless, you are slamming the door in the face of God.

Charles Allen

Without the certainty of His resurrection, we would come to the end of this life without hope, with nothing to anticipate except despair and doubt. But because He lives, we rejoice, knowing soon we will meet our Savior face to face, and the troubles and trials of this world will be behind us.

BILL BRIGHT

The Lord Himself has laid the foundation of His people's hopes. We must determine if our hopes are built on this foundation.

C. H. SPURGEON

Hope can give us life. It can provide energy that would otherwise do us in completely if we tried to operate in our own strength.

BARBARA JOHNSON

TODAY'S PRAYER

Dear Lord, let my hopes always reside in you.
If I become discouraged, let me turn to you.
If I grow tired, let me find strength in you.
You are my Father, and I will place my faith,
my trust, and my hopes in you.

Amen.

The Temptation to Judge

When they kept on questioning him,
he straightened up and said to them,
"Let any one of you who is without sin
be the first to throw a stone at her."

JOHN 8:7

The warning of Matthew 7:1 is clear: "Do not judge, or you too will be judged." Yet even the most devoted Christians may fall prey to a powerful yet subtle temptation: the temptation to judge others. But as obedient followers of Christ, we are commanded to refrain from such behavior.

As Jesus came upon a young woman who had been condemned by the Pharisees, he spoke not only to the crowd that was gathered there, but also to all generations when he warned, "Let any one of you who is without sin be the first to throw a stone at her" (John 8:7). Christ's message is clear, and it applies not only to the Pharisees of ancient times, but also to us.

Forget the faults of others by remembering your own.

JOHN BUNYAN

Only Christ can free us from the prison of legalism, and then only if we are willing to be freed.

MADELEINE L'ENGLE

Judging draws the judgment of others.

CATHERINE MARSHALL

Being critical of others, including God, is one way we try to avoid facing and judging our own sins.

WARREN WIERSBE

TODAY'S PRAYER

Dear Lord, sometimes I am quick to judge others.
But you have commanded me not to judge. Keep me
mindful, Father, that when I judge others,
I am living outside of your will for my life.
You have forgiven me, Lord. Let me forgive others,
let me love them, and let me help them . . .
without judging them.

Amen.

THE WORLD . . . AND YOU

Do not conform to the pattern of this world,
but be transformed by the renewing of your mind.
Then you will be able to test and approve what God's
will is—his good, pleasing and perfect will.

ROMANS 12:2

We live in the world, but we must not worship it. Our duty is to place God first and everything else second. But because we are fallible beings with imperfect faith, placing God in his rightful place is often difficult. In fact, at every turn, or so it seems, we are tempted to do otherwise.

The 21st-century world is a noisy, distracting place filled with countless opportunities to stray from God's will. The world seems to cry, "Worship me with your time, your money, your energy, and your thoughts!" But God commands otherwise. He commands us to worship him and him alone; everything else must be secondary.

The only ultimate disaster that can befall us, I have come to realize, is to feel ourselves to be home on earth.

MAX LUCADO

Because the world is deceptive, it is dangerous. The world can even deceive God's own people and lead them into trouble.

WARREN WIERSBE

Our fight is not against any physical enemy; it is against organizations and powers that are spiritual. We must struggle against sin all our lives, but we are assured we will win.

CORRIE TEN BOOM

A fish would never be happy living on land, because it was made for water. An eagle could never feel satisfied if it wasn't allowed to fly. You will never feel completely satisfied on earth, because you were made for more.

RICK WARREN

TODAY'S PRAYER

Dear Lord, I am an imperfect human being living in an imperfect world. Direct my path far from the temptations and distractions of this world, and let me follow in the footsteps of your Son today and forever.

Amen.

USING GOD'S GIFTS

*Each of you should use whatever gift you have
received to serve others, as faithful stewards
of God's grace in its various forms.*

1 PETER 4:10

All men possess special gifts—bestowed from the Father above—and you are no exception. But, your gift is no guarantee of success; it must be cultivated and nurtured; otherwise, it will go unused . . . and God's gift to you will be squandered.

Today, make a promise to yourself that you will earnestly seek to discover the talents that God has given you. Then, nourish those talents and make them grow. Finally, vow to share your gifts with the world for as long as God gives you the power to do so. After all, the best way to say "Thank you" for God's gifts is to use them.

When God crowns our merits, he is crowning nothing other than his gifts.

ST. AUGUSTINE

God is still in the process of dispensing gifts, and He uses ordinary individuals like us to develop those gifts in other people.

HOWARD HENDRICKS

Almighty God created us, redeemed us, called us, endowed us with gifts and abilities and perceptions. To demean the gift is to insult the Giver.

PENELOPE STOKES

There's a unique sense of fulfillment that comes when we submit our gifts to God's use and ask him to energize them in a supernatural way—and then step back to watch what he does. It can be the difference between merely existing in black and white and living a life in full, brilliant color.

LEE STROBEL

TODAY'S PRAYER

Dear Lord, let me use my gifts, and let me help others discover theirs. Your gifts are priceless and eternal. May we, your children, use them to the glory of your kingdom, today and forever.

Amen.

YOU ARE BLESSED

*I will make them and the places surrounding my hill
a blessing. I will send down showers in season;
there will be showers of blessing.*

EZEKIEL 34:26

I f you sat down and began counting your blessings, how long would it take? A very, very long time! Your blessings include life, freedom, family, friends, talents, and possessions—for starters. But, your greatest blessing—a gift that is yours for the asking—is God's gift of salvation through Christ Jesus.

Today, begin making a list of your blessings. You most certainly will not be able to make a complete list, but take a few moments and jot down as many blessings as you can. Then give thanks to the giver of all good things— God. His love for you is eternal, as are his gifts. And it's never too soon—or too late—to offer him thanks.

When God blesses us, He expects us to use those blessings to bless the lives of others.

JIM GALLERY

God wants his people to earnestly seek his will and to pray for it, and thus to become agents of the blessing God brings.

JAMES MONTGOMERY BOICE

Think of the blessings we so easily take for granted: Life itself; preservation from danger; every bit of health we enjoy; every hour of liberty; the ability to see, to hear, to speak, to think, and to imagine all this comes from the hand of God.

BILLY GRAHAM

TODAY'S PRAYER

Lord, I have more blessings than I can possibly count; make me mindful of your precious gifts. You have cared for me, Lord, and you have saved me. I will give thanks and praise you always. Today, let me share your blessings with others, just as you first shared them with me.

Amen.

CHEERFULNESS 101

All the days of the oppressed are wretched,
but the cheerful heart has a continual feast.

PROVERBS 15:15

C hrist promises us lives of abundance and joy, but he does not force his joy upon us. We must claim his joy for ourselves, and when we do, Jesus, in turn, fills our spirits with his power and his love. Few things in life are sadder, or, for that matter, more absurd, than a grumpy Christian.

How can we receive from Christ the joy that is rightfully ours? By giving him what is rightfully his: our hearts and our souls.

When we earnestly commit ourselves to the Savior of humankind, when we place Jesus at the center of our lives and trust him as our personal Savior, he will transform us, not just for today, but for all eternity. Then we, as God's children, can share Christ's joy and his message with a world that needs both.

Christ can put a spring in your step and a thrill in your heart. Optimism and cheerfulness are products of knowing Christ.

BILLY GRAHAM

When I think of God, my heart is so full of joy that the notes leap and dance as they leave my pen; and since God has given me a cheerful heart, I serve him with a cheerful spirit.

FRANZ JOSEPH HAYDN

Cheerfulness sharpens the edge and removes the rust from the mind. A joyous heart supplies oil to our inward machinery, and makes the whole of our powers work with ease and efficiency; hence it is of the utmost importance that we maintain a contented, cheerful, genial disposition."

JAMES H. AUGHEY

TODAY'S PRAYER

Dear Lord, you have given me so many reasons to be happy, and I want to be a cheerful Christian. Today and every day, I will do my best to share my happiness with my family and my friends.

Amen.

LET GOD DECIDE

In their hearts humans plan their course,
but the LORD establishes their steps.

PROVERBS 16:9

The world will often lead you astray, but God will not. His counsel leads you to himself, which, of course, is the path he has always intended for you to take. Are you facing a difficult decision, a troubling circumstance, or a powerful temptation? If so, it's time to step back, to stop focusing on the world, and to focus, instead, on the will of your Father in heaven.

Everyday living is an exercise in decision-making. Today and every day you must make choices—choices about what you will do, what you will worship, and how you will think. When in doubt, make choices that you sincerely believe will bring you to a closer relationship with God. And if you're uncertain of your next step, pray about it. When you do, answers will come—the right answers for you.

God always gives His best to those who leave the choice with Him.

JIM ELLIOT

There is no need to fear the decisions of life when you know Jesus Christ, for His name is Counselor.

WARREN WIERSBE

As we trust God to give us wisdom for today's decisions, He will lead us a step at a time into what He wants us to be doing in the future.

THEODORE EPP

I don't doubt that the Holy Spirit guides your decisions from within when you make them with the intention of pleasing God. The error would be to think that He speaks only within, whereas in reality He speaks also through Scripture, the Church, Christian friends, and books.

C. S. LEWIS

TODAY'S PRAYER

Lord, help me to make decisions that are pleasing to you. Help me to be honest, patient, thoughtful, and obedient. And above all, help me to follow the teachings of Jesus, not just today, but every day.

Amen.

The Remedy for Uncertainty

*[Jesus] replied, "You of little faith, why are you
so afraid?" Then he got up and rebuked the winds
and the waves, and it was completely calm.*

Matthew 8:26

Sometimes, like Jesus' disciples, we feel threatened
by the storms of life. During these moments, when
our hearts are flooded with uncertainty, we must
remember that God is not simply near; he is here.

Have you ever felt your faith in God slipping away? If
so, you are in good company. Even the most faithful
Christians suffer occasional bouts of discouragement and
doubt. But even when you feel far removed from God,
God never leaves your side. He is always with you, always
willing to calm the storms of life. When you sincerely
seek his presence—and when you genuinely seek to
establish a deeper, more meaningful relationship with his
Son—God will calm your fears, answer your prayers, and
restore your soul.

We basically have two choices to make in dealing with the mysteries of God. We can wrestle with Him or we can rest in Him.

CALVIN MILLER

There is a difference between doubt and unbelief. Doubt is a matter of mind: we cannot understand what God is doing or why He is doing it. Unbelief is a matter of will: we refuse to believe God's Word and obey what He tells us to do.

WARREN WIERSBE

Mark it down. God never turns away the honest seeker. Go to God with your questions. You may not find all the answers, but in finding God, you know the One who does.

MAX LUCADO

TODAY'S PRAYER

Dear God, sometimes this world can be a puzzling place, filled with uncertainty and doubt. When I am unsure of my next step, keep me mindful that you are always near and that you can overcome any challenge. With your love and your power, Father, I can live courageously and faithfully, today and every day. Amen.

THANKSGIVING YES . . . ENVY NO!

*Refrain from anger and turn from wrath; do not fret—
it leads only to evil.*

PSALM 37:8

As the recipient of God's grace, you have every reason to celebrate life. After all, God has promised you the opportunity to receive his abundance and his joy—in fact, you have the opportunity to receive those gifts right now. But if you allow envy to gnaw away at the fabric of your soul, you'll find that joy remains elusive.

So do yourself an enormous favor: Rather than succumbing to the sin of envy, focus on the marvelous things that God has done for you—starting with Christ's sacrifice.

Thank the giver of all good gifts, and keep thanking him for the wonders of his love and the miracles of his creation. Count your own blessings and let your neighbors count theirs. It's the godly way to live.

As a moth gnaws a garment, so does envy consume a man.

St. John Chrysostom

How can you possess the miseries of envy when you possess in Christ the best of all portions?

C. H. Spurgeon

When you worry about what you don't have, you won't be able to enjoy what you do have.

Charles Swindoll

Too many Christians envy the sinners their pleasure and the saints their joy because they don't have either one.

Martin Luther

Today's Prayer

Dear Lord, deliver me from the needless pain of envy. You have given me countless blessings. Let me be thankful for the gifts I have received, and let me never be resentful of the gifts you have given others.

Amen.

WALKING IN HIS FOOTSTEPS

*I have set you an example that you should do
as I have done for you.*

JOHN 13:15

As citizens of a fast-changing world, we face challenges that sometimes leave us feeling overworked, over-committed, and overwhelmed. But God has different plans for us. He intends that we slow down long enough to praise him and to glorify his Son.

Each day, we are confronted with countless opportunities to serve God and to follow in the footsteps of his Son. When we do, our heavenly Father guides our steps and blesses our endeavors. He lifts our spirits and enriches our lives.

Today provides a glorious opportunity to place yourself in the service of the One who is the giver of all blessings. May you seek his will, may you trust his Word, and may you walk in the footsteps of his Son.

Christ is to be sought and bought with any pains, at any price; we cannot buy this gold too dear. He is a jewel worth more than a thousand worlds. Get him, and get all; miss him and miss all.

HOMAS BROOKS

To walk out of His will is to walk into nowhere.

C. S. LEWIS

WWJD = Walking With Jesus Daily.

ANONYMOUS

Imagine the spiritual strength the disciples drew from walking hundreds of miles with Jesus . . . (2 John 4).

JIM MAXWELL

TODAY'S PRAYER

Dear Jesus, because I am your disciple,
I will trust you, I will obey your teachings,
and I will share your good news.
You have given me life abundant and life eternal,
and I will follow you today and forever.

Amen.

In His Hands

Do not boast about tomorrow,
for you do not know what a day may bring.

O ur world unfolds according to God's plans, not our wishes. Thus, boasting about future events is to be avoided by those who acknowledge God's sovereignty over all things. The old saying is both familiar and true: "Man proposes and God disposes."

Are you planning for a better tomorrow for yourself and your family? If so, you are to be congratulated. God rewards forethought in the same way that he often punishes impulsiveness. But as you make your plans, do so with humility, with gratitude, and with trust in your heavenly Father. His hand directs the future; to think otherwise is both arrogant and naïve.

Tomorrow's history has already been written—at the name of Jesus every knee must bow.

PAUL E. KAUFFMAN

Our future may look fearfully intimidating, yet we can look up to the Engineer of the Universe, confident that nothing escapes His attention or slips out of the control of those strong hands.

ELISABETH ELLIOT

Hoping for a good future without investing in today is like a farmer waiting for a crop without ever planting any seed.

JOHN MAXWELL

That we may not complain of what is, let us see God's hand in all events; and, that we may not be afraid of what shall be, let us see all events in God's hand.

MATTHEW HENRY

TODAY'S PRAYER

Dear Lord, as I look to the future, I will place my trust in you. If I become discouraged, I will turn to you. If I am weak, I will seek strength in you. You are my Father, and I will place my hope, my trust, and my faith in you.

Amen.

OBEY AND BE BLESSED

We know that we have come to know him
if we keep his commands.

1 JOHN 2:3

O swald Chambers, the author of the Christian classic devotional text, *My Utmost for His Highest*, advised, "Never support an experience which does not have God as its source, and faith in God as its result." These words serve as a powerful reminder that, as Christians, we are called to walk with God and obey his commandments. God gave us his commandments for a reason: So that we might obey them and be blessed.

We live in a world that presents us with countless temptations to stray far from God's path. But, when confronted with sin, we Christians have clear instructions: Walk—or better yet—run in the opposite direction.

To yield to God means to belong to God, and to belong to God means to have all His infinite power. To belong to God means to have all.

HANNAH WHITALL SMITH

Faith, as Paul saw it, was a living, flaming thing leading to surrender and obedience to the commandments of Christ.

A. W. TOZER

Let us remember therefore this lesson: That to worship our God sincerely we must evermore begin by hearkening to His voice, and by giving ear to what He commands us. For if every man goes after his own way, we shall wander. We may well run, but we shall never be a whit nearer to the right way, but rather farther away from it.

JOHN CALVIN

TODAY'S PRAYER

Lord, let me live by your commandments and let me help others do the same. Give me the wisdom to walk righteously in the footsteps of your Son, dear Father. And let me place my trust in you, today and forever.

Amen.

THE LOVE OF MONEY

For the love of money is a root of all kinds of evil.
Some people, eager for money, have wandered from
the faith and pierced themselves with many griefs.

1 TIMOTHY 6:10

Our society is in love with money and the things that money can buy. God is not. God cares about people, not possessions, and so must we. We must, to the best of our abilities, love our neighbors as ourselves. And we must, to the best of our abilities, resist the mighty temptation to place possessions ahead of people.

Money, in and of itself, is not evil; worshipping money is. So today, as you prioritize matters of importance for you and yours, remember that God is almighty, but the dollar is not. If we worship God, we are blessed. But if we worship "the almighty dollar," we are inevitably punished because of our misplaced priorities—and our punishment inevitably comes sooner rather than later.

If the glories of heaven were more real to us, if we lived less for material things and more for things eternal and spiritual, we would be less easily disturbed in this present life.

BILLY GRAHAM

Christians have become victims of one of the most devious plots Satan ever created—the concept that money belongs to us and not to God.

LARRY BURKETT

Greed is enslaving. The more you have, the more you want—until eventually avarice consumes you.

KAY ARTHUR

TODAY'S PRAYER

Dear Lord, I will earn money and I will use money, but I will not worship money. Give me the wisdom and the discipline to be a responsible steward of my financial resources, and let me use those resources for the glory of your kingdom.

Amen.

He Offers Peace

Peace I leave with you; my peace I give you. I do not give to you as the world gives. Do not let your hearts be troubled and do not be afraid.

JOHN 14:27

The beautiful words of John 14:27 remind us that Jesus offers us peace, not as the world gives, but as he alone gives. Have you found the genuine peace that can be yours through Jesus Christ? Or are you still rushing after the illusion of "peace and happiness" that the world promises but cannot deliver?

Today, as a gift to yourself, to your family, and to your friends, claim the inner peace that is your spiritual birthright—the peace of Jesus Christ. It is offered freely; it has been paid for in full; it is yours for the asking. So ask. And then share.

God cannot give us happiness and peace apart from Himself, because it is not there. There is no such thing.

C. S. LEWIS

Peace does not mean to be in a place where there is no noise, trouble, or hard work. Peace means to be in the midst of all those things and still be calm in your heart.

CATHERINE MARSHALL

Christ alone can bring lasting peace—peace with God— peace among men and nations—and peace within our hearts.

BILLY GRAHAM

God's peace is like a river, not a pond. In other words, a sense of health and well-being, both of which are expressions of the Hebrew shalom, can permeate our homes even when we're in white-water rapids.

BETH MOORE

TODAY'S PRAYER

Dear Lord, I will open my heart to you.
And I thank you, God, for your love,
for your peace, and for your Son.

Amen.

Constant Praise

*Through Jesus, therefore, let us continually offer
to God a sacrifice of praise—the fruit of lips
that openly profess his name.*

Hebrews 13:15

Sometimes, we allow ourselves to become so preoccupied with the demands of daily life that we forget to say "Thank you" to the giver of all good gifts. But the Bible makes it clear: It pays to praise God.

Worship and praise should be a part of everything we do. Otherwise, we quickly lose perspective as we fall prey to the demands of the moment.

Do you sincerely desire to be a worthy servant of the One who has given you eternal love and eternal life? Then praise him for who he is and for what he has done for you. Praise him all day long, every day, for as long as you live . . . and then for all eternity.

Be not afraid of saying too much in the praises of God; all the danger is of saying too little.

Matthew Henry

Worship is an act which develops feelings for God, not a feeling for God which is expressed in an act of worship. When we obey the command to praise God in worship, our deep, essential need to be in relationship with God is nurtured.

EUGENE PETERSON

Praise God from whom all blessings flow. Praise Him all creatures here below. Praise Him above ye heavenly host. Praise Father, Son, and Holy Ghost.

THOMAS KEN

TODAY'S PRAYER

Heavenly Father, I come to you today with hope in my heart and praise on my lips. I place my trust in you, dear Lord, knowing that with you as my protector, I have nothing to fear. I thank you, Lord, for your grace, for your love, and for your Son.

Amen.

The Shepherd's Gift

*My cup overflows. Surely your goodness and love will
follow me all the days of my life, and I will dwell in
the house of the LORD forever.*

PSALM 23:5-6

When we entrust our hearts and our days to the One who created us, we experience abundance through the grace and sacrifice of his Son. But, when we turn our thoughts and direct our energies away from God's commandments, we inevitably forfeit the spiritual abundance that might otherwise be ours.

Do you sincerely seek the riches that our Savior offers to those who give themselves to him? Then follow him completely and obey him without reservation. When you do, you will receive the love and the abundance that he has promised. Seek first the salvation that is available through a personal relationship with Jesus Christ, and then claim the joy, the peace, and the spiritual abundance that the Good Shepherd offers his sheep.

God is the giver, and we are the receivers. And His richest gifts are bestowed not upon those who do the greatest things, but upon those who accept His abundance and His grace.

HANNAH WHITALL SMITH

Instead of living a black-and-white existence, we'll be released into a Technicolor world of vibrancy and emotion when we more accurately reflect His nature to the world around us.

BILL HYBELS

People, places, and things were never meant to give us life. God alone is the author of a fulfilling life.

GARY SMALLEY & JOHN TRENT

TODAY'S PRAYER

Good Shepherd, thank you for the abundant life that is mine through Christ Jesus. Guide me according to your will, and help me to be a worthy servant in all that I say and do. Give me courage, Lord, to claim the rewards you have promised, and when I do, let the glory be yours.

Amen.

HE RENEWS OUR STRENGTH

*Do you not know? Have you not heard? The Lord is the
everlasting God the Creator of the ends of the earth.
He will not grow tired or weary, and his understanding
no one can fathom. He gives strength to the weary and
increases the power of the weak. Even youths grow tired
and weary, and young men stumble and fall; but those
who hope in the Lord will renew their strength.
They will soar on wings like eagles; they will run and
not grow weary, they will walk and not be faint.*

ISAIAH 40:28–31

When we genuinely lift our hearts and prayers to God, he
renews our strength.

- Are you almost too weary to lift your head? Then
  bow it. Offer your concerns and your fears to your
  Father in heaven. He is always at your side, offering
  his love and his strength.

- Are you troubled or anxious? Take your anxieties to
  God in prayer.

- Are you weak or worried? Delve deeply into God's
  Holy Word and sense his presence in the quiet
  moments of the day.

- Are you spiritually exhausted? Call upon fellow
  believers to support you, and call upon Christ to
  renew your spirit and your life.

Your Savior will never let you down. To the contrary, he will always lift you up if you ask him to. So what, dear friend, are you waiting for?

God specializes in taking bruised, soiled, broken, guilty, and miserable vessels and making them whole, forgiven, and useful again.

CHARLES SWINDOLL

The amazing thing about Jesus is that He doesn't just patch up our lives, He gives us a brand-new sheet, a clean slate to start over, all new.

GLORIA GAITHER

TODAY'S PRAYER

Heavenly Father, sometimes I am troubled, and sometimes I grow weary. When I am weak, Lord, give me strength. When I am discouraged, renew me. When I am fearful, let me feel your healing touch. Let me always trust in your promises, Lord, and let me draw strength from those promises and from your unending love.

Amen.

SHARING THE GOOD NEWS

*For Christ did not send me to baptize, but to preach
the gospel—not with wisdom and eloquence,
lest the cross of Christ be emptied of its power.*

1 CORINTHIANS 1:17

In his second letter to Timothy, Paul offers a message to believers of every generation when he writes, "For the Spirit God gave us does not make us timid" (1:7). Paul's meaning is crystal clear: When sharing our testimonies, we, as Christians, must be courageous, forthright, and unashamed.

We live in a world that desperately needs the healing message of Christ Jesus. Every believer, each in his or her own way, bears a personal responsibility for sharing that message. If you are a believer in Christ, you know how he has touched your heart and changed your life.

Now it's your turn to share the good news with others. And remember: Today is the perfect time to share your testimony because tomorrow may quite simply be too late.

There is nothing anybody else can do that can stop God from using us. We can turn everything into a testimony.

CORRIE TEN BOOM

To stand in an uncaring world and say, "See, here is the Christ" is a daring act of courage.

CALVIN MILLER

All of God's people are ministers; a few are Ministers with a capital *M*. We are either good ministers or bad ministers; but ministers we are, and as ministers we shall be judged by the Lord on the Last Day.

WARREN WIERSBE

TODAY'S PRAYER

Lord, the life that I live and the words that I speak
will tell the world how I feel about you.
Today and every day, let my testimony be worthy of
you. Let my words be sure and true,
and let my actions point others to you.

Amen.

TEMPORARY SETBACKS

A time to weep and a time to laugh,
a time to mourn and a time to dance.

ECCLESIASTES 3:4

The occasional disappointments and failures of life are inevitable. Such setbacks are simply the price that we must occasionally pay for our willingness to take risks as we follow our dreams. But even when we encounter bitter disappointments, we must never lose faith.

When we encounter the inevitable difficulties of life here on earth, God stands ready to protect us. Our responsibility, of course, is to ask him for protection. When we call upon him in heartfelt prayer, he will answer—in his own time and according to his own plan—and he will heal us.

And, while we are waiting for God's plans to unfold and for his healing touch to restore us, we can be comforted in the knowledge that our Creator can overcome any obstacle, even if we cannot.

The enemy of our souls loves to taunt us with past failures, wrongs, disappointments, disasters, and calamities. And if we let him continue doing this, our life becomes a long and dark tunnel, with very little light at the end.

CHARLES SWINDOLL

God is a specialist; He is well able to work our failures into His plans. Often the doorway to success is entered through the hallway of failure.

ERWIN LUTZER

God sometimes permits us to experience humiliating defeats in order to test our faith and to reveal to us what's really going on in our hearts.

WARREN WIERSBE

TODAY'S PRAYER

Dear Lord, even when I'm afraid of failure, give me the courage to try. Remind me that with you by my side, I really have nothing to fear. So today, Father, I will live courageously as I place my faith in you.

Amen.

THE MORNING WATCH

He wakens me morning by morning,
wakens my ear to listen like one being instructed.
The Sovereign LORD has opened my ears.

ISAIAH 50:4–5

Each new day is a gift from God, and if you are wise, you will spend a few quiet moments each morning thanking the giver.

Warren Wiersbe writes, "Surrender your mind to the Lord at the beginning of each day." And that's sound advice. When you begin each day with your head bowed and your heart lifted, you are reminded of God's love, his protection, and his commandments. Then, you can align your priorities for the coming day with the teachings and commandments that God has placed upon your heart.

So, if you've acquired the unfortunate habit of trying to squeeze God into the corners of your life, it's time to reshuffle the items on your to-do list by placing God first. And if you haven't already done so, form the habit of spending quality time with your Father in heaven. He deserves it . . . and so do you.

I suggest you discipline yourself to spend time daily in a systematic reading of God's Word. Make this "quiet time" a priority that nobody can change.

WARREN WIERSBE

Knowing God involves an intimate, personal relationship that is developed over time through prayer and getting answers to prayer, through Bible study and applying its teaching to our lives, through obedience and experiencing the power of God, through moment-by-moment submission to Him that results in a moment-by-moment filling of the Holy Spirit.

ANNE GRAHAM LOTZ

If thou may not continually gather thyself together, do it some time at least, once a day, morning or evening.

THOMAS À KEMPIS

TODAY'S PRAYER

Lord, help me to hear your direction for my life in the quiet moments of each day. Let everything that I say and do be in your perfect will.

Amen.

WISDOM IN A DONUT SHOP

Choose my instruction instead of silver,
knowledge rather than choice gold,
for wisdom is more precious than rubies,
and nothing you desire can compare with her.

PROVERBS 8:10–11

Many years ago, this rhyme was posted on the wall of a small donut shop:

As you travel through life brother,
Whatever be your goal,
Keep your eye upon the donut,
And not upon the hole.

These simple words remind us of a profound truth: We should spend more time looking at the things we have, not worrying about the things we don't have.

When you think about it, you've got more blessings than you can count. So make it a habit to thank God for the gifts he's given you, not the gifts you wish he'd given you.

We may run, walk, stumble, drive, or fly, but let us never lose sight of the reason for the journey, or miss a chance to see a rainbow on the way.

GLORIA GAITHER

The people whom I have seen succeed best in life have always been cheerful and hopeful people who went about their business with a smile on their faces.

CHARLES KINGSLEY

No Christian can be a pessimist, for Christianity is a system of radical optimism.

WILLIAM RALPH INGE

TODAY'S PRAYER

Dear Lord, I will look for the best in other people, I will expect the best from you, and I will try my best to do my best—today and every day.

Amen.

PLEASING GOD

So we make it our goal to please him,
whether we are at home in the body or away from it.

2 CORINTHIANS 5:9

When God made you, he equipped you with an array of talents and abilities that are uniquely yours. It's up to you to discover those talents and to use them. But sometimes the world will encourage you to do otherwise.

At times, society will attempt to cubbyhole you, to standardize you, and to make you fit into a particular, preformed mold. Sometimes, because you're an imperfect human being, you may become so wrapped up in meeting society's expectations that you fail to focus on God's expectations. To do so is a mistake of major proportions—don't make it.

Who will you try to please today: God or man? Your primary obligation is not to please imperfect men and women. Your obligation is to strive diligently to meet the expectations of an all-knowing and perfect God. Trust him always. Love him always. Praise him always. And seek to please him. Always.

It is impossible to please God doing things motivated by and produced by the flesh.

BILL BRIGHT

Whether we think of, or speak to, God, whether we act or suffer for him, all is prayer when we have no other object than his love and the desire of pleasing him.

JOHN WESLEY

All our offerings, whether music or martyrdom, are like the intrinsically worthless present of a child, which a father values indeed, but values only for the intention.

C. S. LEWIS

TODAY'S PRAYER

Dear Lord, today I will honor you with my thoughts, my actions, and my prayers. I will seek to please you, and I will strive to serve you.
Your blessings are as limitless as your love.
And because I have been so richly blessed,
I will worship you, Father, with thanksgiving in my heart and praise on my lips, this day and forever.

Amen.

A God-Made Man

Humility is the fear of the LORD;
its wages are riches and honor and life.

PROVERBS 22:4

We have heard the phrase on countless occasions: *He's a self-made man.* In truth, none of us are self-made. We all owe countless debts that we can never repay.

Our first debt, of course, is to our Father in heaven—Who has given us everything that we are and will ever be—and to his Son who sacrificed his own life so that we might live eternally. We are also indebted to ancestors, parents, teachers, friends, spouses, family members, coworkers, fellow believers . . . and the list, of course, goes on.

Most of us, it seems, are more than willing to stick out our chests and say, "Look at me; I did that!" But in our better moments, in the quiet moments when we search the depths of our own hearts, we know better. Whatever "it" is, God did that. And he deserves the credit.

Humility expresses a genuine dependency on God and others.

CHARLES STANLEY

Jesus had a humble heart. If He abides in us, pride will never dominate our lives.

BILLY GRAHAM

If you know who you are in Christ, your personal ego is not an issue.

BETH MOORE

TODAY'S PRAYER

Heavenly Father, Jesus clothed himself with humility when he chose to leave heaven and come to earth to live and die for all creation. Christ is my master and my example. Clothe me with humility, Lord, so that I might be more like your Son.

Amen.

WHEN PEOPLE BEHAVE BADLY

Do not make friends with a hot-tempered person,
do not associate with one easily angered, or you may
learn their ways and get yourself ensnared.

PROVERBS 22:24-25

Face it: Sometimes people can be rude—very rude. When other people are unkind to you, you may be tempted to strike back, either verbally or in some other way. Don't do it! Instead, remember that God corrects other people's behaviors in his own way, and he doesn't need your help (even if you're totally convinced that he does).

So, when other people behave cruelly, foolishly, or impulsively—as they will from time to time—don't be hotheaded. Instead, speak up for yourself as politely as you can, and walk away. Then, forgive everybody as quickly as you can, and leave the rest up to God.

We are all fallen creatures and all very hard to live with.

C. S. LEWIS

Bear with the faults of others as you would have them bear with yours.

PHILLIPS BROOKS

A keen sense of humor helps us to overlook the unbecoming, understand the unconventional, tolerate the unpleasant, overcome the unexpected, and outlast the unbearable.

BILLY GRAHAM

From what does such contrariness arise in habitually angry people, but from a secret cause of too high an opinion of themselves so that it pierces their hearts when they see any man esteem them less than they esteem themselves? An inflated estimation of ourselves is more than half the weight of our wrath.

ST. THOMAS MORE

TODAY'S PRAYER

Dear Lord, sometimes people behave badly. When other people upset me, help me to calm myself down, and help me forgive them as quickly as I can.

Amen.

Acceptance Today

*I have learned to be content
whatever the circumstances.*

Philippians 4:11

Are you embittered by a personal tragedy that you did not deserve and cannot understand? If so, it's time to accept the unchangeable past and to have faith in the promise of tomorrow. It's time to trust God completely—and it's time to reclaim the peace—his peace—that can and should be yours.

On occasion, you will be confronted with situations that you simply don't understand. But God does. And he has a reason for everything that he does.

God doesn't explain himself in ways that we, as mortals with limited insight and clouded vision, can comprehend. So, instead of understanding each and every aspect of God's unfolding plan for our lives and our universe, we must be satisfied to trust him completely. We cannot know God's motivations; nor can we understand his actions. We can, however, trust him, and we must.

Faith is the willingness to receive whatever he wants to give, or the willingness not to have what he does not want to give.

ELISABETH ELLIOT

The key to contentment is to consider. Consider who you are and be satisfied with that. Consider what you have and be satisfied with that. Consider what God's doing and be satisfied with that.

LUCI SWINDOLL

I have held many things in my hands, and I have lost them all; but whatever I have placed in God's hands, that I still possess.

CORRIE TEN BOOM

TODAY'S PRAYER

Heavenly Father, thank you for the abundant life that is mine through Christ. Give me courage, Lord, to claim the spiritual riches that you have promised, and lead me according to your plan for my life, today and always.

Amen.

Choosing Wisely

*The wisdom that comes from heaven is first of all
pure; then peace-loving, considerate, submissive,
full of mercy and good fruit, impartial and sincere.*

James 3:17

Because we are creatures of free will, we make choices—lots of them. When we make choices that are pleasing to our heavenly Father, we are blessed. When we make choices that cause us to walk in the footsteps of God's Son, we enjoy the abundance that Christ has promised to those who follow him. But when we make choices that are displeasing to God, we sow seeds that have the potential to bring forth a bitter harvest.

Today, as you encounter the challenges of everyday living, you will make hundreds of choices. Choose wisely. Make your thoughts and your actions pleasing to God. And remember: Every choice that is displeasing to him is the wrong choice—no exceptions.

God expresses His love in giving us the freedom
to choose.

Charles Stanley

Life is a series of choices between the bad, the good, and the best. Everything depends on how we choose.

VANCE HAVNER

We are either the masters or the victims of our attitudes. It is a matter of personal choice. Who we are today is the result of choices we made yesterday. Tomorrow, we will become what we choose today. To change means to choose to change.

JOHN MAXWELL

Good and evil both increase at compound interest. That is why the little decisions you and I make every day are of such infinite importance.

C. S. LEWIS

TODAY'S PRAYER

Dear Lord, today I will focus my thoughts on your will for my life. I will strive to make decisions that are pleasing to you, and I will strive to follow in the footsteps of your Son.

Amen.

CONFIDENT CHRISTIANITY

You have been my hope, Sovereign LORD,
my confidence since my youth.

PSALM 71:5 NASB

Sometimes, even the most devout Christians can become discouraged. Discouragement, however, is not God's way; he is a God of possibility, not negativity. We Christians have many reasons to be confident. God is in his heaven; Christ has risen; and we are the sheep of his flock.

Are you a confident Christian? You should be. God's grace is eternal and his promises are clear. So count your blessings, not your hardships. And live courageously. God is the giver of all things good, and he watches over you today and forever.

God's omniscience can instill you with a supernatural confidence that can transform your life.

BILL HYBELS

If we indulge in any confidence that is not grounded on the Rock of Ages, our confidence is worse than a dream; it will fall on us and cover us with its ruins, causing sorrow and confusion.

C. H. SPURGEON

Jesus gives us the ultimate rest, the confidence we need, to escape the frustration and chaos of the world around us.

BILLY GRAHAM

TODAY'S PRAYER

Lord, when I place my confidence in the things
of this earth, I will be disappointed.
But, when I put my confidence in you, I am secure.
In every aspect of my life,
Father, let me place my hope and my trust in your
infinite wisdom and your boundless grace.

Amen.

GENUINE CONTENTMENT

The LORD gives strength to his people;
the LORD blesses his people with peace.

PSALM 29:11

Everywhere we turn, or so it seems, the world promises us contentment and happiness. But the contentment that the world offers is fleeting and incomplete. Thankfully, the contentment that God offers is all encompassing and everlasting.

Happiness depends less upon our circumstances than upon our thoughts. When we turn our thoughts to God, to his gifts, and to his glorious creation, we experience the joy that God intends for his children. But, when we focus on the negative aspects of life—or when we disobey God's commandments—we cause ourselves needless suffering.

Do you sincerely want to be a contented Christian? Then set your mind and your heart upon God's love and his grace . . . and let him take care of the rest.

Contentment is not escape from battle, but rather an abiding peace and confidence in the midst of battle.

WARREN WIERSBE

The secret of contentment in the midst of change is found in having roots in the changeless Christ—the same yesterday, today and forever.

ED YOUNG

Contentment is something we learn by adhering to the basics—cultivating a growing relationship with Jesus Christ, living daily, and knowing that Christ strengthens us for every challenge.

CHARLES STANLEY

I believe that in every time and place it is within our power to acquiesce in the will of God—and what peace it brings to do so!

ELISABETH ELLIOT

TODAY'S PRAYER

Dear Lord, you offer me contentment and peace; let me accept your peace. Help me to trust your Word, to follow your commandments, and to welcome the peace of Jesus into my heart, today and forever.

Amen.

A BOOK UNLIKE ANY OTHER

I am not ashamed of the gospel, because it is the power of God that brings salvation to everyone who believes: first to the Jew, then to the Gentile.

ROMANS 1:16

God's Word is unlike any other book. A. W. Tozer wrote, "The purpose of the Bible is to bring men to Christ, to make them holy and prepare them for heaven. In this it is unique among books, and it always fulfills its purpose."

George Müller observed, "The vigor of our spiritual lives will be in exact proportion to the place held by the Bible in our lives and in our thoughts." As Christians, we are called upon to study God's Holy Word and then to share it with the world.

The Bible is a priceless gift, a tool for Christians to use as they share the good news of their Savior, Christ Jesus. Too many Christians, however, keep their spiritual tool kits tightly closed and out of sight. Jonathan Edwards advised, "Be assiduous in reading the Holy Scriptures. This is the fountain whence all knowledge in divinity must be derived. Therefore let not this treasure lie by you neglected." God's Holy Word is, indeed, a priceless, one-of-a-kind treasure. Handle it with care, but, more importantly, handle it every day.

The instrument of our sanctification is the Word of God. The Spirit of God brings to our minds the precepts and doctrines of truth, and applies them with power. The truth is our sanctifier. If we do not hear or read it, we will not grow in sanctification.

C. H. SPURGEON

I am certain that the Bible is the Word of God. Either it is or it isn't, and either all of it is the Word of God, or we never can be sure of any of it. It is either absolute or obsolete. If we have to start changing this verse, toning down that, apologizing for this and making allowances for that, we might as well give up, so we must take it as it is or leave it alone.

VANCE HAVNER

The Bible is a remarkable commentary on perspective. Through its divine message, we are brought face to face with issues and tests in daily living and how, by the power of the Holy Spirit, we are enabled to respond positively to them.

LUCI SWINDOLL

TODAY'S PRAYER

Dear Lord, the Bible is your gift to me.
Let me use it, let me trust it, and let me obey it,
today and every day that I live. Amen.

SHOUTING THE GOOD NEWS

As you go, proclaim this message:
"The kingdom of heaven has come near."

MATTHEW 10:7

The good news of Jesus Christ should be shouted from the rooftops by believers the world over. But all too often, it is not. For a variety of reasons, many Christians keep their beliefs to themselves, and when they do, the world suffers because of their failure to speak up.

As believers, we are called to share the transforming message of Jesus with our families, with our neighbors, and with the world. Jesus commands us to become fishers of men. And, the time to go fishing is now. We must share the good news of Jesus Christ today—tomorrow may be too late.

God is not saving the world; it is done. Our business is to get men and women to realize it.

OSWALD CHAMBERS

For every believer, the task, or mission, is to lead people to the truth of Jesus Christ.

CHARLES STANLEY

Taking the gospel to people wherever they are—death row, the ghetto, or next door—is frontline evangelism, frontline love. It is our one hope for breaking down barriers and for restoring the sense of community, of caring for one another, that our decadent, impersonalized culture has sucked out of us.

CHUCK COLSON

Christianity spread rapidly during the first century because all Christians saw themselves as responsible for disseminating the gospel.

ERWIN LUTZER

TODAY'S PRAYER

Lord, even if I never leave home, make me a missionary for you. Let me share the good news of your Son, and let me tell of your love and of your grace. Make me a faithful servant for you, Father, now and forever.

Amen.

A Life of Fulfillment

For you, God, tested us; you refined us like silver.
You brought us into prison and laid burdens on our
backs. You let people ride over our heads;
we went through fire and water,
but you brought us to a place of abundance.

PSALM 66:10-12

Everywhere we turn, or so it seems, the world promises fulfillment, contentment, and happiness. But the contentment that the world offers is fleeting and incomplete. Thankfully, the fulfillment that God offers is all encompassing and everlasting.

Sometimes, amid the inevitable hustle and bustle of life here on earth, we can forfeit—albeit temporarily—the joy of Christ as we wrestle with the challenges of daily living. Yet God's Word is clear: Fulfillment through Christ is available to all who seek it and claim it.

Count yourself among that number. Seek first a personal, transforming relationship with Jesus, and then claim the joy, the fulfillment, and the spiritual abundance that the Good Shepherd offers his sheep.

Find satisfaction in him who made you, and only then find satisfaction in yourself as part of his creation.

ST. AUGUSTINE

We are made for God, and nothing less will really satisfy us.

BRENNAN MANNING

Our sense of joy, satisfaction, and fulfillment in life increases, no matter what the circumstances, if we are in the center of God's will.

BILLY GRAHAM

TODAY'S PRAYER

Dear Lord, when I turn my thoughts and prayers
to you, I feel peace and fulfillment.
But sometimes, when I am distracted by the
busyness of the day, fulfillment seems far away.
Today, let me trust your will, let me follow your
commands, and let me accept your peace.

Amen.

GOD IS LOVE

We know and rely on the love God has for us.
God is love. Whoever lives in love lives in God,
and God in them.

1 JOHN 4:16

The Bible makes this promise: God is love. It's a sweeping statement, a profoundly important description of what God is and how God works. God's love is perfect. When we open our hearts to his perfect love, we are touched by the Creator's hand, and we are transformed.

Today, even if you can only carve out a few quiet moments, offer sincere prayers of thanksgiving to your Creator. He loves you now and throughout all eternity. Open your heart to his presence and his love.

The life of faith is a daily exploration of the constant and countless ways in which God's grace and love are experienced.

EUGENE PETERSON

If it is maintained that anything so small as the Earth must, in any event, be too unimportant to merit the love of the Creator, we reply that no Christian ever supposed we did merit it. Christ did not die for men because they were intrinsically worth dying for, but because He is intrinsically love, and therefore loves infinitely.

C. S. LEWIS

Love, for instance, is not something God has which may grow or diminish or cease to be. His love is the way God is, and when He loves He is simply being himself.

A. W. TOZER

TODAY'S PRAYER

Dear God, you are love.
You love me, Father, and I love you.
As I love you more, Lord, I am also able to love my family and friends more. I will be your loving servant, Lord, today and throughout eternity.

Amen.

WE ARE ALL ROLE MODELS

You are the light of the world. A town built on a hill cannot be hidden. In the same way, let your light shine before others, that they may see your good deeds and glorify your Father in heaven.

MATTHEW 5:14,16

Whether we like it or not, we are role models. Hopefully, the lives we lead and the choices we make will serve as enduring examples of the spiritual abundance that is available to all who worship God and obey his commandments.

Ask yourself this question: Are you the kind of role model that you would want to emulate? If so, congratulations. But if certain aspects of your behavior could stand improvement, the best day to begin your self-improvement regimen is this one. Because whether you realize it or not, people you love are watching your behavior, and they're learning how to live. You owe it to them—and to yourself—to live righteously and well.

A man ought to live so that everybody knows he is a Christian, and most of all, his family ought to know.

D. L. MOODY

Let us preach you, Dear Jesus, without preaching, not by words but by our example, by the casting force, the sympathetic influence of what we do, the evident fullness of the love our hearts bear to You. Amen.

MOTHER TERESA

Our walk counts far more than our talk, always!

GEORGE MÜLLER

TODAY'S PRAYER

Dear Lord, help me be an honorable role model to others. Let the things that I say and the things that I do show everyone what it means to be a follower of your Son.

Amen.

HEEDING GOD'S CALL

One thing I do: Forgetting what is behind and straining toward what is ahead, I press on toward the goal to win the prize for which God has called me heavenward in Christ Jesus.

PHILIPPIANS 3:13–14

It is vitally important that you heed God's call. In John 15:16, Jesus says, "You did not choose me, but I chose you and appointed you so that you might go and bear fruit—fruit that will last." In other words, you have been called by Christ, and now, it is up to you to decide precisely how you will answer.

Have you already found your special calling? If so, you're a very lucky person. If not, keep searching and keep praying until you discover it. And remember this: God has important work for you to do—work that no one else on earth can accomplish but you.

The place where God calls you is the place where your deep gladness and the world's deep hunger meet.

FREDERICK BUECHNER

Faith does not concern itself with the entire journey. One step is enough.

Mrs. Charles E. Cowman

When you become consumed by God's call on your life, everything will take on new meaning and significance. You will begin to see every facet of your life, including your pain, as a means through which God can work to bring others to Himself.

Charles Stanley

The Bible teaches that God has considered man a working partner.

Billy Graham

Today's Prayer

Heavenly Father, you have called me to your kingdom work, and I acknowledge that calling. In these quiet moments before this busy day unfolds, I come to you. I will study your Word and seek your guidance. Give me the wisdom to know your will for my life and the courage to follow wherever you may lead me, today and forever.

Amen.

BECOMING WISE

Walk with the wise and become wise.

PROVERBS 13:20

Wisdom does not spring up overnight—it takes time. To become wise, we must seek God's wisdom and live according to his Word. And, we must not only learn the lessons of the Christian life, we must also live by them.

Do you seek to live a life of righteousness and wisdom? If so, you must study the ultimate source of wisdom—the Word of God. You must seek out worthy mentors and listen carefully to their advice. You must associate, day in and day out, with godly men and women. And, you must act in accordance with your beliefs. When you do these things, you will become wise . . . and you will be a blessing to your friends, to your family, and to the world.

The theme of Proverbs is wisdom, the right use of knowledge. It enables you to evaluate circumstances and people and make the right decisions in life.

WARREN WIERSBE

When you and I are related to Jesus Christ, our strength and wisdom and peace and joy and love and hope may run out, but his life rushes in to keep us filled to the brim. We are showered with blessings, not because of anything we have or have not done, but simply because of Him.

ANNE GRAHAM LOTZ

Wisdom is the right use of knowledge. To know is not to be wise. Many men know a great deal, and are all the greater fools for it. There is no fool so great a fool as a knowing fool. But to know how to use knowledge is to have wisdom.

CHARLES SPURGEON

TODAY'S PRAYER

Dear Lord, when I depend upon the world's wisdom, I make many mistakes. But when I trust in your wisdom, I build my life on a firm foundation. Today and every day I will trust your Word and follow it, knowing that the ultimate wisdom is your wisdom and the ultimate truth is your truth.

Amen.

Beyond Worry

Blessed is the one who trusts in the Lord.

PROVERBS 16:20

Because we are imperfect human beings, we worry. Even though we are Christians who have been given the assurance of salvation—even though we are Christians who have received the promise of God's love and protection—we find ourselves fretting over the countless details of everyday life. Jesus understood our concerns when he spoke the reassuring words found in Matthew 6:25, "Therefore I tell you, do not worry about your life . . ."

As you consider the promises of Jesus, remember that God still sits in his heaven and you are his beloved child. Then, perhaps, you will worry a little less and trust God a little more, and that's as it should be because God is trustworthy . . . and you are protected.

We are not called to be burden-bearers, but cross-bearers and light-bearers. We must cast our burdens on the Lord.

CORRIE TEN BOOM

I've read the last page of the Bible. It's all going to turn out all right.

BILLY GRAHAM

It is not work that kills, but worry. And, it is amazing how much wear and tear the human mind and spirit can stand if it is free from friction and well-oiled by the Spirit.

VANCE HAVNER

It has been well said that no man ever sank under the burden of the day. It is when tomorrow's burden is added to the burden of today that the weight is more than a man can bear. Never load yourselves so, my friends. If you find yourselves so loaded, at least remember this: it is your own doing, not God's. He begs you to leave the future to Him and mind the present.

GEORGE MACDONALD

TODAY'S PRAYER

Forgive me, Lord, when I worry. Worry reflects a lack of trust in you. Help me to work, Lord, and not to worry. And, keep me mindful, Father, that nothing, absolutely nothing, will happen this day that you and I cannot handle together.

Amen.

MAKING PEACE WITH YOUR PAST

The LORD says, "Forget the former things; do not dwell on the past. See, I am doing a new thing! Now it springs up; do you not perceive it? I am making a way in the wilderness and streams in the wasteland."

ISAIAH 43:18–19

Because you are human, you may be slow to forget yesterday's disappointments. But, if you sincerely seek to focus your hopes and energies on the future, then you must find ways to accept the past, no matter how difficult it may be to do so.

Have you been able to make peace with your past? If so, congratulations. But, if you are mired in the quicksand of regret, it's time to plan your escape. How can you do so? By accepting what has been and by trusting God for what will be.

So, if you have not yet made peace with the past, today is the day to declare an end to all hostilities. When you do, you can then turn your thoughts to the wondrous promises of God and to the glorious future that he has in store for you.

Our yesterdays teach us how to savor our todays and tomorrows.

PATSY CLAIRMONT

The wise man gives proper appreciation in his life to his past. He learns to sift the sawdust of heritage in order to find the nuggets that make the current moment have any meaning.

GRADY NUTT

Shake the dust from your past, and move forward in His promises.

KAY ARTHUR

The pages of your past cannot be rewritten, but the pages of your tomorrows are blank.

ZIG ZIGLAR

TODAY'S PRAYER

Heavenly Father, free me from anger, resentment, and envy. When I am bitter, I cannot feel the peace that you intend for my life. Keep me mindful that forgiveness is your commandment, and help me accept the past, treasure the present, and trust the future . . . to you. Amen.

His Perspective . . . and Yours

Since, then, you have been raised with Christ,
set your hearts on things above, where Christ is,
seated at the right hand of God.

Colossians 3:1

If a temporary loss of perspective has left you worried, exhausted, or both, it's time to readjust your thought patterns. Negative thoughts are habit-forming; thankfully, so are positive ones. With practice, you can form the habit of focusing on God's priorities and your own possibilities. When you do, you'll soon discover that you will spend less time fretting about your challenges and more time praising God for his gifts.

When you call upon the Lord and prayerfully seek his will, he will give you wisdom and perspective. When you make God's priorities your priorities, he will direct your steps and calm your fears. So today and every day hereafter, pray for a sense of balance and perspective. And remember: No problems are too big for God—and that includes yours.

Attitude is the mind's paintbrush; it can color any situation.

Barbara Johnson

Instead of being frustrated and overwhelmed by all that is going on in our world, go to the Lord and ask Him to give you His eternal perspective.

KAY ARTHUR

When we look at the individual parts of our lives, some things appear unfair and unpleasant. When we take them out of the context of the big picture, we easily drift into the attitude that we deserve better, and the tumble down into the pit of pride begins.

SUSAN HUNT

TODAY'S PRAYER

Lord, sometimes, the world's perspective can lead me astray. Sometimes I become confused; sometimes, in the busyness of my daily life, I lose perspective. Help me, Lord, to see the world through your eyes. Give me guidance, wisdom, and perspective. Lead me according to your plan for my life and according to your commandments. And keep me ever mindful, Father, that your reality is the ultimate reality, and that your truth is the ultimate truth, now and forever.

Amen.

SOLVING PROBLEMS

*The righteous person may have many troubles,
but the LORD delivers him from them all.*

PSALM 34:19

Life is an exercise in problem-solving. The question
is not whether we will encounter problems; the
real question is how we will choose to address
them. When it comes to solving the problems of everyday
living, we often know precisely what needs to be done, but
we may be slow in doing it—especially if what needs to be
done is difficult or uncomfortable for us. So we put off till
tomorrow what should be done today.

The words of Psalm 34 remind us that the Lord solves
problems for people who do what is right. And usually,
doing "what is right" means doing the uncomfortable
work of confronting our problems sooner rather than
later. So let the problem-solving begin . . . now.

We are all faced with a series of great opportunities,
brilliantly disguised as unsolvable problems. Unsolvable
without God's wisdom, that is.

CHARLES SWINDOLL

You've got problems; I've got problems; all God's children have got problems. The question is how are you going to deal with them?

JOHN MAXWELL

I choose joy. I will refuse the temptation to be cynical; cynicism is the tool of a lazy thinker. I will refuse to see people as anything less than human beings, created by God. I will refuse to see any problem as anything less than an opportunity to see God.

MAX LUCADO

TODAY'S PRAYER

Lord, sometimes my problems are simply too big
for me, but they are never too big for you.
Let me turn my troubles over to you, Lord,
and let me trust in you today and for all eternity.

Amen.

Beyond Bitterness

Do not take revenge, my dear friends,
but leave room for God's wrath, for it is written:
"It is mine to avenge; I will repay," says the LORD.

ROMANS 12:19

Bitterness is a spiritual sickness. It will consume your soul; it is dangerous to your emotional health. It can destroy you if you let it . . . so don't let it!

If you are caught up in intense feelings of anger or resentment, you know all too well the destructive power of these emotions. How can you rid yourself of these feelings? First, you must prayerfully ask God to cleanse your heart. Then, you must learn to catch yourself whenever thoughts of bitterness or hatred begin to attack you. Your challenge is this: You must learn to resist negative thoughts before they hijack your emotions.

Matthew 5:22 teaches us that if we judge our brothers and sisters, we, too, will be subject to judgement. Let us refrain, then, from judging our neighbors. Instead, let us forgive them and love them, while leaving their judgement to a far more capable authority—The One who sits on his throne in heaven.

Bitterness is a spiritual cancer, a rapidly growing malignancy that can consume your life. Bitterness cannot be ignored but must be healed at the very core, and only Christ can heal bitterness.

BETH MOORE

Revenge is the raging fire that consumes the arsonist.

MAX LUCADO

Be patient and understanding. Life is too short to be vengeful or malicious.

PHILLIPS BROOKS

Forgiveness is the key that unlocks the door of resentment and the handcuffs of hate. It is a power that breaks the chains of bitterness and the shackles of selfishness.

CORRIE TEN BOOM

TODAY'S PRAYER

Dear Lord, free me from the poison of bitterness
and the futility of blame. Let me turn away
from destructive emotions so that I may know
the perfect peace and the spiritual abundance
that can, and should, be mine.
Amen.

UNBENDING TRUTH

Each of you must put off falsehood
and speak truthfully to your neighbor,
for we are all members of one body.

EPHESIANS 4:25

Oswald Chambers advised, "Never support an experience which does not have God as its source, and faith in God as its result." These words serve as a powerful reminder that as Christians we are each called to walk with God and to obey his commandments. But, we live in a world that presents us with countless temptations to wander far from God's path. These temptations have the potential to destroy us, in part, because they cause us to be dishonest with ourselves and with others.

Dishonesty is a habit. Once we start bending the truth, we're likely to keep bending it. A far better strategy, of course, is to acquire the habit of being completely forthright with God, with other people, and with ourselves.

Honesty is also a habit, a habit that pays powerful dividends for those who place character above convenience. So, the next time you're tempted to bend the truth—or to break it—ask yourself this simple question: "What does God want me to do?" Then listen carefully to your conscience. When you do, your actions will be honorable, and your character will take care of itself.

Right actions done for the wrong reason do not help to build the internal quality of character called a "virtue," and it is this quality or character that really matters.

C. S. Lewis

God never called us to naïveté. He called us to integrity. The biblical concept of integrity emphasizes mature innocence not childlike ignorance.

Beth Moore

A solid trust is based on a consistent character.

John Maxwell

Today's Prayer

Heavenly Father, help me see the truth,
help me speak the truth, and help me live the truth—
today and every day of my life.

Amen.

A Series of Choices

*Seek first his kingdom and his righteousness,
and all these things will be given to you as well.*

MATTHEW 6:33

Your life is a series of choices. From the instant you wake up in the morning until the moment you nod off to sleep at night, you make countless decisions:

- Decisions about the things you do

- Decisions about the words you speak

- Decisions about the way that you choose to direct your thoughts

As a believer who has been transformed by the love of Jesus, you have every reason to make wise choices. But sometimes, when the daily grind threatens to grind you up and spit you out, you may make choices that are displeasing to God. When you do, you'll pay a price because you'll forfeit the happiness and the peace that might otherwise have been yours.

So as you pause to consider the kind of Christian that you are—and the kind of Christian that you want to become—ask yourself whether you're sitting on the fence or standing in the light. The choice is yours . . . and so are the consequences.

There may be no trumpet sound or loud applause when we make a right decision, just a calm sense of resolution and peace.

GLORIA GAITHER

The greatest choice any man makes is to let God choose for him.

VANCE HAVNER

Every day, I find countless opportunities to decide whether I will obey God and demonstrate my love for Him or try to please myself or the world system. God is waiting for my choices.

BILL BRIGHT

TODAY'S PRAYER

Heavenly Father, I have many choices to make. Help me choose wisely as I follow in the footsteps of your only begotten Son.

Amen.

Focusing on God

*Do not worry about tomorrow,
for tomorrow will worry about itself.
Each day has enough trouble of its own.*

Matthew 6:34

All of us may find our courage tested by the inevitable disappointments and tragedies of life. After all, ours is a world filled with uncertainty, hardship, sickness, and danger. Trouble, it seems, is never too far from the front door.

When we focus on our fears and our doubts, we may find many reasons to lie awake at night and fret about the uncertainties of the coming day. A better strategy, of course, is to focus instead on our God.

God is as near as your next breath, and he is in control. He offers salvation to all his children, including you. God is your shield and your strength; you are his forever. So don't focus your thoughts upon the fears of the day. Instead, trust God's plan and his eternal love for you. And remember: God is good, and he has the last word.

Ignoring Him by neglecting prayer and Bible reading will cause you to doubt.

Anne Graham Lotz

His hand on me is a father's hand, gently guiding and encouraging. His hand lets me know he is with me, so I am not afraid.

MARY MORRISON SUGGS

Whether our fear is absolutely realistic or out of proportion in our minds, our greatest refuge is Jesus Christ.

LUCI SWINDOLL

Fear and doubt are conquered by a faith that rejoices. And faith can rejoice because the promises of God are as certain as God Himself.

KAY ARTHUR

TODAY'S PRAYER

Your Word reminds me, Lord, that even when I walk through the valley of the shadow of death, I need fear no evil for you are with me, and you comfort me. Thank you, Lord, for a perfect love that casts out fear. Let me live courageously and faithfully this day and every day.

Amen.

COMMISSIONED TO WITNESS

Go and make disciples of all nations, baptizing them in the name of the Father and of the Son and of the Holy Spirit, and teaching them to obey everything I have commanded you. And surely I am with you always, to the very end of the age.

MATTHEW 28:19–20

After his resurrection, Jesus addressed his disciples. As recorded in Matthew 28:19-20, Christ instructed his followers to share his message with the world. This "Great Commission" applies to Christians of every generation, including our own.

As believers, we are called to share the good news of Jesus with our families, with our neighbors, and with the world. Christ commanded his disciples to become fishers of men. We must do likewise, and we must do so today. Tomorrow may be too late.

Witnessing is not something that we do for the Lord; it is something that He does through us if we are filled with the Holy Spirit.

WARREN WIERSBE

Our commission is quite specific. We are told to be His witness to all nations. For us, as His disciples, to refuse any part of this commission frustrates the love of Jesus Christ, the Son of God.

CATHERINE MARSHALL

In their heart of hearts, I think all true followers of Christ long to become contagious Christians. Though unsure about how to do so or the risks involved, deep down they sense that there isn't anything as rewarding as opening a person up to God's love and truth.

BILL HYBELS

TODAY'S PRAYER

Heavenly Father, every man and woman, every boy and girl is your child. You desire that all your children know Jesus as their Lord and Savior. Father, let me be part of your Great Commission. Let me give, let me pray, and let me go out into this world so that I might be a fisher of men . . . for you.

Amen.

OTHER RESOURCES FROM
STEPHEN ARTERBURN

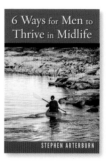

7 Ways to Choose Healing

Learn how to make choices to ensure you experience the healing that God, in his eternal purpose, has for you.

Paperback, 124 pages, 4.5 x 6.5

ISBN: 9781628624298
PRODUCT CODE: 4139X

6 Ways for Men to Thrive in Midlife

Midlife doesn't have to be a crisis of identity or a failure in self-confidence. Midlife can be a season of discovering how your past years and present situation are the very material to make an exciting future.

Paperback, 124 pages, 4.5 x 6.5

ISBN: 9781628624489
PRODUCT CODE: 4149X

NEW LIFE MINISTRIES, founded by Steve Arterburn, exists to go into life's hardest places with you. Visit NewLife.com today to see how we can help. Be sure to check our live call-in times for New Life Live!, or call 800-HELP-4-ME to hear the next available time. We want to hear from you!

www.hendricksonrose.com
www.aspirepress.com